The Art of Pickling and Fermentation

Sustainable Food Techniques for Self-Sufficient Living

Sofia Ramirez

Table of Contents

INTRODUCTION

In an era marked by an increasing awareness of environmental sustainability and a desire for self-sufficiency, the art of pickling and fermentation emerges as a timeless practice with profound relevance. Rooted in tradition yet adaptable to modern lifestyles, pickling and fermentation offer a means of preserving food and a gateway to a more sustainable, self-reliant way of life.

"The Art of Pickling and Fermentation" is a guidebook crafted for those seeking to embrace the transformative power of these ancient culinary techniques. Within these pages, we embark on a journey to explore the intricate interplay of flavors, textures, and cultures that define the world of pickling and fermentation. More than mere preservation methods, they are embodiments of resourcefulness, creativity, and respect for the bounty of nature.

At its core, this book celebrates the marriage of tradition and innovation, inviting readers to rediscover the lost art of preserving food while adapting it to the demands of modern living. From tangy sauerkraut to fiery kimchi, from crisp pickles to robust sourdough, the possibilities for culinary exploration are endless. Yet beyond the realm of taste, pickling and fermentation offer many practical benefits, from extending the shelf life of seasonal produce to enhancing the nutritional value of everyday meals.

Moreover, this book is a testament to the profound connection between food and sustainability. By embracing pickling and fermentation, individuals can reduce food waste, minimize reliance on processed goods, and cultivate a deeper appreciation for the rhythms of nature. Whether you're a seasoned homesteader or a novice urban gardener, the principles outlined herein empower you to take control of your food supply, one jar at a time.

"The Art of Pickling and Fermentation" is not just a manual; it's a manifesto for a more sustainable, self-sufficient future. So, join us as we embark on a voyage of discovery, where the humblest of ingredients becomes a canvas for culinary creativity, and every meal is a celebration of resilience and abundance. Welcome to the world of pickling and fermentation — where tradition meets innovation, and sustainability is a way of life.

CHAPTER I

What is Pickling and Fermentation?

Importance of Sustainable Food Techniques

The importance of sustainable food techniques has become an increasingly critical issue in the face of global challenges including climate change, population growth, and diminishing natural resources. As the world grapples with these complex problems, the need for innovative, sustainable approaches to food production and consumption has never been more apparent. Sustainable food techniques encompass a broad range of practices designed to minimize environmental impact, support local economies, and promote the planet's and its inhabitants' health and well-being.

At the heart of sustainable food techniques is the principle of meeting the current generation's needs without sacrificing the ability of generations to come to meet their own. This principle guides efforts to reduce greenhouse gas emissions, conserve water and soil, protect biodiversity, and ensure equitable access to nutritious food. Sustainable agriculture practices, including organic farming, crop rotation, and agroforestry, play a pivotal role in this endeavor. These practices not only help maintain healthy ecosystems but also improve soil fertility and reduce the requirement for chemical fertilizers and pesticides, which can be harmful to the environment and the human health.

Moreover, sustainable food techniques involve a holistic approach encompassing the entire food system, from production and processing to distribution, consumption, and waste management. For instance, embracing local food systems can significantly reduce the carbon footprint connected with long-distance food transportation. It also supports local farmers and communities, fostering resilience in local economies. Similarly, initiatives that encourage the consumption of plant-based diets contribute to reducing the environmental impact of food production, as livestock farming is one of the primary contributors to greenhouse gas emissions and resource depletion.

Another critical aspect of sustainable food techniques is the minimization of food waste. Globally, a significant portion of the food produced is never consumed, resulting in wasteful use of resources and contributing to greenhouse gas emissions from decomposing waste. Strategies to combat food waste include improving food storage and preservation methods, enhancing supply chain efficiencies, and promoting consumer awareness about the significance of reducing waste. These efforts not only help conserve resources but also have the possibility to enhance food security by redistributing surplus food to those in need.

In addition to environmental benefits, sustainable food techniques offer numerous health advantages. Organic and locally sourced foods are often fresher and less likely to consist of harmful pesticides and additives, improving nutrition and health outcomes. Furthermore, sustainable food systems tend to promote diversity in diets, which is essential for nutrition and can help combat the global rise in obesity and diet-related diseases.

The transition to sustainable food techniques also poses challenges, including the need for technological innovation, changes in consumer behavior, and supportive policies and investments. Technological advancements in areas including renewable energy, precision agriculture, and biodegradable packaging can enhance the efficiency and sustainability of food systems. However, widespread adoption of these technologies requires investment and education to ensure that farmers and food producers have the necessary skills and resources.

Consumer behavior is crucial in driving demand for sustainable food products. Increasing awareness and understanding of food choices' environmental and health impacts can encourage more sustainable consumption patterns. This, in turn, can create market incentives for producers to adopt sustainable practices. Governments and policymakers have an important role to play in facilitating this transition through regulations, incentives, and support for research and development in sustainable food technologies.

In conclusion, the importance of sustainable food techniques lies in their potential to address some of the most pressing challenges of our time. We can move towards a more sustainable and equitable food system by adopting practices that prioritize environmental health, support local economies, and promote nutritious diets. The journey towards sustainability requires concerted efforts from individuals, communities, businesses, and governments. It is a complex but necessary endeavor that promises a healthier planet and a better future for all its inhabitants. As we look forward, it is clear that sustainable food techniques will be pivotal in shaping the way we grow, consume, and think about food in the years to come.

Brief Overview of Pickling and Fermentation

The ancient practices of pickling and fermentation have been integral to human civilization for thousands of years, serving as a means to preserve food, enhance its flavor, and boost its nutritional value. These techniques, while simple in their essence, embody a complex interplay of biology and chemistry that transforms the original ingredients into products with distinct tastes, textures, and health benefits. This section provides a brief overview of pickling and fermentation, exploring their historical roots, processes, and their roles in various cultures worldwide.

Pickling is known as a method of preserving food in an acidic medium, typically vinegar, or through the natural fermentation process where lactic acid is produced, making the environment hostile to food-spoiling bacteria. The origins of pickling are as old as agriculture itself, with evidence suggesting that ancient Mesopotamians pickled cucumbers as early as 2400 B.C. This technique was not only a necessity before the advent of modern refrigeration but also a way to ensure a supply of vegetables out of season. Pickled foods such as cucumbers, carrots, onions, and even fruits are common across many cultures, each adding its unique blend of spices and flavorings to create a diverse array of pickled delicacies.

Fermentation, conversely, is a metabolic process that produces chemical changes in organic substrates through the action of enzymes. In the context of food, it commonly refers to the conversion of carbohydrates to alcohols, carbon dioxide, or organic acids using microorganisms—yeasts or bacteria—under anaerobic conditions. Fermentation has been used to produce many of the world's staple foods and beverages, including bread, cheese, yogurt, wine, beer, and soy sauce. Like pickling, fermentation not only extends the shelf life of food but also enhances its nutritional and organoleptic properties. The art of fermentation is celebrated in various cultures, each boasting a rich tradition of fermented foods that are integral to their culinary heritage.

The pickling process begins with submerging the food in a brining solution or covering it with salt to draw out moisture—a crucial step that inhibits the growth of spoilage-causing microorganisms. The food is then submerged in vinegar or a similar acidic solution, which creates an environment where bacteria cannot thrive. Alternatively, in the case of naturally fermented pickles, the food is kept in a saltwater brine, encouraging the growth of lactic acid bacteria that ferment the sugars in the food into lactic acid. This not only preserves the food but also can lead to the development of intricate flavors and probiotics, which are helpful for gut health.

While it may occur naturally, fermentation is often initiated and controlled by adding specific strains of bacteria or yeast, depending on the desired product. The process is carefully monitored to ensure optimal conditions for the particular microorganisms involved. For example, making yogurt involves fermenting milk with a culture of Lactobacillus bulgaricus as well as Streptococcus thermophilus, while brewing beer starts with the fermentation of malted barley by yeast. The end products of fermentation are diverse, reflecting the myriad ways in which this technique can be applied, each with its unique flavor, texture, and nutritional profile.

Both pickling and fermentation offer significant health benefits. Many pickled and fermented foods contain vitamins, minerals, and antioxidants. The fermentation process, in particular, can increase the bioavailability of nutrients, making them more accessible for the body to absorb. Additionally, fermented foods are known for their probiotic content and beneficial bacteria that are crucial in maintaining gut health and enhancing the immune system. These health benefits, combined with the longevity and enhanced flavors that these methods impart to food, underscore the continued relevance of pickling and fermentation in contemporary diets.

Culturally, pickling and fermentation are more than just food preservation techniques; they are traditions passed down through generations, often imbued with significant cultural and symbolic meanings. In Korea, for example, kimchi—a fermented vegetable dish, typically made with cabbage and radishes—is a national staple that is present at virtually every meal. Similarly, in Eastern Europe, pickled cucumbers and fermented cabbage (sauerkraut) are deeply ingrained in the culinary traditions. These foods are enjoyed for their taste and health benefits and their cultural significance, serving as a link to history, tradition, and identity.

In conclusion, the practices of pickling and fermentation represent a fascinating blend of science, tradition, and art. By soaking foods in acidic solutions or allowing them to ferment, humans have developed an array of flavors and textures that enrich our diets and contribute to our health. These methods, rooted in the necessity of preserving food, have evolved into cherished culinary practices that celebrate the diversity of human culture and ingenuity. As we continue to explore and appreciate the complexity of pickling and fermentation, these ancient techniques remind us of our connection to the past and our ongoing quest for sustenance, flavor, and well-being.

Benefits of Pickling and Fermentation for Self-Sufficient Living

The practices of pickling and fermentation are ancient food preservation techniques that have seen a resurgence in recent years, particularly among individuals and communities striving for self-sufficient living. This revival is not merely a nod to tradition but a recognition of the myriad benefits these methods offer regarding sustainability, health, and culinary diversity. In a world where the virtues of self-reliance and sustainability are increasingly prized, pickling and fermentation stand out as valuable skills that can enhance food security, reduce waste, and contribute to a healthier diet. This section explores the benefits of pickling and fermentation for self-sufficient living, emphasizing their role in sustainable practices, nutritional enhancement, and the promotion of food diversity.

Self-sufficient living involves minimizing reliance on commercial food production and distribution systems, aiming instead to produce and preserve one's own food. In this context, pickling and fermentation are invaluable techniques. They allow individuals to extend the shelf life of fruits, vegetables, and even meats without the need for refrigeration. This is particularly advantageous for those living off-grid or in areas where electricity is unreliable or expensive. By preserving seasonal produce, individuals can enjoy a varied diet year-round, reducing the need to purchase out-of-season produce that is often expensive and less nutritious due to long transport distances.

Moreover, these preservation methods align with sustainable living principles by reducing food waste—a significant issue in global food systems. Parts of produce that might otherwise be discarded, such as vegetable peels or overripe fruits, can be transformed into delicious, nutritious foods through pickling and fermentation. This not only conserves resources but also fosters a culture of resourcefulness and appreciation for the value of food.

From a nutritional standpoint, pickled and fermented foods are powerhouses of health benefits. For instance, the fermentation process increases the bioavailability of nutrients, which in turn makes it simpler for the body to absorb them. The helpful bacteria known as probiotics are found in abundance in fermented foods. Probiotics play an essential role in the maintenance of intestinal health. There is a correlation between a healthy microbiome in the gut and a number of health benefits, including improved immune function, improved digestion, and a decreased chance of developing chronic diseases. In addition, fermentation has the potential to raise the levels of particular vitamins, such as vitamin K2 and B vitamins, and to enhance the nutritional profile of meals as a whole.

For individuals pursuing self-sufficient living, cultivating a diet rich in pickled and fermented foods can also contribute to food diversity and culinary innovation. These methods offer endless possibilities for flavor combinations and can transform simple ingredients into complex, flavorful dishes. This not only enriches the dining experience but also encourages a more profound connection with the food we eat, as individuals become more involved in the process of growing, preserving, and preparing their meals. Furthermore, mastering these techniques can create unique products tailored to personal tastes and dietary needs, further enhancing the self-sufficient lifestyle.

The cultural aspect of pickling and fermentation also contributes to the richness of self-sufficient living. These techniques are steeped in tradition and offer a way to connect with cultural heritage and pass on knowledge to future generations. They foster a sense of community as individuals share recipes, techniques, and the fruits of their labor. This communal aspect is a cornerstone of self-sufficient living, where sharing resources and knowledge strengthens social bonds and supports a collective move towards more sustainable lifestyles.

Economically, pickling and fermentation can lead to significant savings for those committed to self-sufficient living. Individuals can prevent the high costs of purchasing out-of-season or imported foods by preserving seasonal produce at its peak. Additionally, these methods can transform inexpensive, bulk ingredients into various products, thereby diversifying one's diet without needing specialty items. The initial investment in materials for pickling and fermentation is relatively low and pays off in the long run, as these tools and containers can be reused indefinitely.

Despite their many benefits, pickling and fermentation also require a willingness to learn and experiment. Success in these endeavors comes from understanding the basic principles of the processes, including the importance of cleanliness, the correct ratios of salt or acid, and the optimal conditions for fermentation. However, the learning curve is part of the appeal, offering a hands-on way to engage with food and understand its transformation from raw ingredients to preserved goods.

In conclusion, the benefits of pickling and fermentation for self-sufficient living are manifold, encompassing sustainability, nutrition, culinary diversity, cultural richness, and economic savings. These age-old techniques offer a practical and enjoyable means to enhance food security, improve health, and foster a more profound connection with the natural world. As more individuals seek ways to live more sustainably and independently, pickling and fermentation stand out as essential skills that not only preserve food but also preserve a way of life that values resourcefulness, health, and community. In embracing these practices, one steps into a tradition that has nourished humans for millennia, armed with the knowledge and skills to nourish oneself and one's community in the years to come.

CHAPTER II

Understanding Pickling

History and Origins of Pickling

The history of pickling and its beginnings may be traced back thousands of years, making it one of the ancient methods of food preservation that humanity is aware of. Over the course of human history, this time-honored method, which entails preserving food in an acidic liquid or through fermentation, has been an essential component in the formation of culinary traditions and the preservation of cultural heritage all over the world. Not only has the process of pickling made it possible for humans to keep food for longer periods of time, particularly during times of scarcity, but it has also contributed to the richness and variety of cuisines around the world, making it an intriguing topic for historical research.

There are as many different civilizations that have adopted and adapted the pickled procedure as there are different origins of pickling. Cucumbers, which are indigenous to India, were among the first foods to be pickled, according to the evidence that implies the development of the art of pickling began approximately 4,000 years ago. The major objective of pickling was to preserve food for eating during times of the year that were not in season as well as for long travels, particularly those via sea. The ancient Mesopotamians are attributed with one of the oldest recorded occurrences of pickling, which indicates the technique's significance in the earliest urban civilizations. This particular instance dates back to 2400 B.C.

In a short amount of time, the practice of pickling spread to other regions, notably Egypt, where it eventually formed an essential component of the cuisine. In addition to pickling cucumbers, the Egyptians also preserved lemons, onions, and a variety of other fruits and vegetables by employing brine, which is a saltwater solution. The food was not only preserved via this approach, but it was also infused with flavors that the ancient Egyptians placed a high value on. Pickling gained even more popularity during the time of the Greeks and Romans, who recognized the health benefits of pickling in addition to its ability to preserve something. They preserved a variety of things, including fish and meats, by pickling them in vinegar. These techniques were described by authors such as Cato and Columella, who emphasized the significance of pickling in the diet of soldiers and sailors.

Adding another layer of complexity to the procedure was the introduction of pickling techniques to Asia. The skill of pickling vegetables and fruits in brine or rice wine has developed into a rich culinary legacy in China, with documents reaching back to 1100 B.C. as evidence of its development. As a result of this practice, a wide range of pickled foods have emerged, many of which continue to be popular in contemporary Chinese cuisine. In a similar vein, the practise of creating kimchi, which entails fermenting vegetables with a combination of flavors, has been an integral component of the Korean diet for hundreds of years. Kimchi is not only a cultural icon that symbolizes the history and identity of the nation, but it is also a tribute to the culinary expertise of fermentation that the Koreans have achieved.

The practice of pickling was adapted and improved upon upon its arrival in Europe, which marked the beginning of the pickling process. As a result of their ability to last for a long time and the simplicity with which they could be moved, pickled foods became an essential component of the diet all throughout Europe during the Middle Ages. A vast variety of pickled foods, such as olives in the Mediterranean region and herring in Northern Europe, came into existence as a result of the extensive use of vinegar, which was initially introduced by the Romans. In the course of the Renaissance period, there was a rise in the popularity of pickling as a component of the culinary arts. During this time, chefs experimented with a wide range of spices and vinegar in order to create gourmet pickled treat.

The importance of pickling stretched far beyond the realm of culinary traditions; it was also an essential component in the process of exploration and commerce. During the Age of Discovery, the ability to store food for extended periods of time was a critical factor in the success of long-distance naval missions. The consumption of pickled foods was an essential source of nourishment for sailors, since it helped to lower the likelihood of scurvy and other ailments that were brought on by vitamin deficiencies. Pickling techniques have expanded all over the world, which is a monument to the significance of pickling in global exploration and trade. Pickled foods have become a frequent component in the diets of people living on different continents.

Native Americans in the Americas had their own customs about the fermentation and preservation of food, which were adapted and improved upon by European settlers. These customs were passed down from one generation to another generation. The pickling recipes and techniques that the settlers brought with them were incorporated into the local food and traditions once they arrived. This confluence resulted in the development of distinctive pickling techniques and flavors that have become fundamental components of American cuisine. Some examples of these are relishes, pickled peppers, and pickled cucumbers.

The art of pickling is currently undergoing a rebirth, which coincides with an increasing interest in traditional methods of food preservation and the health advantages associated with making use of these methods. Pickling is a modern trend that celebrates the rich flavors and probiotic properties that pickled foods offer. This movement embraces both the old techniques of fermentation and the usage of vinegar. There is a growing demand for fermented foods and artisanal pickles, which reflects a desire to reestablish a connection with ancient culinary practices and to take pleasure in the distinctive flavors and health benefits that pickling offers.

In conclusion, the history of pickling and its origins are a tribute to the inventiveness of past civilizations and their significance in the formation of culinary traditions all across the world. Pickling has evolved from its humble beginnings in ancient Mesopotamia and India to its part in global exploration and the fusion of civilizations. Pickling has surpassed its original purpose as a means of food preservation to become a highly regarded culinary skill. Not only does the act of pickling reflect the history of human civilization, but it also continues to develop, which contributes to the enhancement of our diets and strengthens our connection to our cultural heritage. In the process of continuing to investigate and develop new approaches within the field of pickling, we pay homage to the time-honored customs that have provided sustenance to humanity for millennia.

Basic Principles of Pickling

The art of pickling, which is a procedure that is entrenched in tradition and history, acts as a bridge through which traditional culinary practices can be connected to contemporary table settings. This time-honored method, which includes preserving food in an acidic liquid or through fermentation, embodies a set of concepts that are both straightforward and profound. In addition to ensuring the safety and lifespan of preserved foods, these fundamental principles of pickling also enhance the flavors of the foods, which is why pickled goods are such a well-liked staple in the pantries of consumers all over the world. Pickling is an old culinary art that is explored in this section, which goes into the fundamental notions of pickling, including the science, techniques, and cultural importance that lie behind it.

Pickling is based on the fundamental premise of being able to create an environment in which harmful bacteria are unable to thrive, which ultimately results in the preservation of the food. The introduction of acid, which is often in the form of vinegar, or fermentation, in which naturally occurring carbohydrates are transformed into acid by means of helpful bacteria, are both methods that are utilized to accomplish this goal. It is because of the acidic atmosphere that the development of bacteria that cause food to go bad is successfully inhibited, which guarantees that the food will continue to be safe for ingestion for further time periods.

The choice of the medium for pickling is the first principle that must be adhered to in the pickling process. Vinegar-based pickling, also known as rapid pickling, is the method that requires the least amount of effort. All that is required is the food to be submerged in a mixture of vinegar, water, and salt. Sugar and spices are frequently added for flavoring purposes. Because of the high concentration of acetic acid that it contains, vinegar serves as a preservative. The fermentation-based pickling method, on the other hand, makes use of brines made of saltwater to promote the growth of lactic acid bacteria. These bacteria naturally ferment the sugars that are present in the food, which results in the production of lactic acid as a reaction byproduct. However, in addition to imparting a characteristic sour flavor and having the potential to give probiotic benefits, this lactic acid serves a preservation role that is comparable to that of vinegar.

The second principle discusses the significance of the salt and sugar that are used in the pickling process. When it comes to pickling that is based on fermentation, salt is an essential component since it functions as a selective agent that encourages the development of beneficial bacteria while inhibits the growth of dangerous bacteria. The amount of salt that is present in the brine might change based on the recipe and the output that is sought; however, it is essential for establishing the appropriate circumstances and conditions for fermentation. On the other hand, sugar is frequently added to vinegar pickles in order to counteract the acidity and for the purpose of adding taste. Sugar has the potential to supply the bacteria that are responsible for fermentation with additional food, which in turn helps to facilitate the creation of lactic acid.

The use of spices and flavorings is yet another key element that is involved in the pickling process. Pickled items are characterized by their particular flavors, which are achieved via the incorporation of various herbs, spices, and other flavorings. Dill, mustard seeds, garlic, and peppercorns are only few of the traditional spices that are utilized in the process of pickling various foods. Additionally, some of these components, such as mustard seeds, include antibacterial qualities that can further assist in the process of preservation. These ingredients are not only used for flavor.

The selection of the produce or food that will be pickled is quite important as well. Pickling should ideally be done using fresh, high-quality ingredients that are free from bruises or blemishes. This is due to the fact that the quality of the raw materials utilized in the production process has a major influence on the quality of the items that are ultimately manufactured. Pickled vegetables and fruits are the most popular kind of pickled foods; however, meats, eggs, and even dairy products can be pickled if the necessary processes are used.

During the pickling process, the importance of maintaining a clean environment cannot be emphasized. It is necessary to properly clean and, in some instances, sterilize all of the equipment, containers, and utensils that are utilized in the pickling process. This prevents any microorganisms that are not wanted from contaminating the pickling process, which could cause the food to go bad or pose a risk to the health of the consumer. Jars made of glass are frequently used for pickling since they do not react with the acidic contents and can be sterilized with relative ease.

When it comes to the pickling process, temperature and time are also quite important components. Quick pickles can be made in a matter of hours or days, depending on the recipe, and are often preserved in the refrigerator to prevent any bacterial development from occurring. On the other hand, fermented pickles require additional time because the fermentation process takes place at room temperature over the course of several days or weeks. After that, the product is transferred to a cooler storage location in order to slow the fermentation process and maintain the tastes.

Finally, the art of pickling is characterized by the presence of the principle of patience. There is no way to speed up the process, particularly when it involves fermentation-based pickling. It takes time for flavors to develop and for textures to change, and the end result is frequently a product that is significantly superior to its fresh counterpart in terms of both flavor and nutritional value. There are various ways in which the act of pickling can be seen as a practice of mindfulness and respect for the process that is determined by nature.

In conclusion, the fundamental principles of pickling involve an array of factors to take into account, ranging from the selection of the preserving method and the components to the careful attention paid to cleanliness, temperature, and timing. This time-honored procedure offers more than simply a means of preservation; it also offers a canvas for culinary creativity, a tool for improving nutrition, and a connection to cultural customs that are practiced all over the world. It is possible to unlock the full potential of pickling by adhering to these fundamental principles, which will allow one to create delicacies that are not only delicious to the palate but also helpful to one's health and well-being. The fundamental principles of pickling continue to act as our compass as we continue to investigate and experiment within this time-honored tradition. These principles continue to guarantee the safety, quality, and flavor of the foods that we preserve.

Equipment and Ingredients Needed

The art of pickling is a culinary tradition cherished across cultures, offering a way to preserve the bounty of gardens and markets for enjoyment year-round. This process, which can transform a wide array of ingredients into tangy, savory, or sweet delights, relies on a combination of simple yet specific equipment and ingredients. Understanding the essentials needed for pickling is crucial for both novices and experienced enthusiasts aiming to achieve the best results in their pickling endeavors. This section delves into the critical equipment and ingredients necessary for pickling, shedding light on the importance of each and how they contribute to the successful preservation of foods.

At the heart of the pickling process is the equipment used to prepare, contain, and store the pickled goods. The most fundamental piece of equipment is the pickling container, typically glass jars with tight-fitting lids. Glass is preferred for its non-reactive nature, ensuring that it doesn't impart any off-flavors to the pickles or degrade over time due to the acidic contents. Jars come in various sizes, and choosing the right size depends on the quantity of food being pickled and the intended use. Lids are equally important; they must seal tightly to prevent contamination and ensure the preservation process remains anaerobic, especially in fermentation-based pickling.

Another essential tool is the wide-mouthed funnel, which facilitates the clean transfer of brine and vegetables into jars, minimizing spills and waste. A ladle or pourable measuring cup is necessary for distributing the pickling liquid accurately and evenly among the jars. Additionally, tongs or jar lifters are invaluable for handling hot jars when sterilizing them or processing pickles in a water bath, ensuring safety and convenience.

Measuring cups and spoons are indispensable for precisely measuring ingredients, crucial in achieving the desired balance of flavors and ensuring the effectiveness of the preservation process. The accuracy of measurements affects the salinity, acidity, and overall taste of the final product. For fermented pickles, a weight to keep vegetables submerged under the brine and an airlock system may be necessary to allow gases to escape while preventing air (and thus, contaminants) from entering.

On the ingredient side, the foundation of pickling lies in the balance of vinegar, water, salt, and sugar. Vinegar, with its high acetic acid content, acts as a preservative and flavoring agent. White distilled vinegar is commonly used for its clear color and neutral flavor, but apple cider, wine, and rice vinegars are also popular for their distinct tastes. The choice of vinegar can significantly influence the flavor profile of the pickled product.

Salt is crucial in pickling for its role in flavor and preservation, especially in fermentation, where it promotes the growth of desirable bacteria while inhibiting harmful ones. It is important to use pickling or canning salt, which is free from iodine and anti-caking agents that can cloud brine or inhibit fermentation. Sugar, while not always necessary, can be included to balance the acidity of the vinegar and add complexity to the flavor of the pickles.

The water used in pickling should be pure and free from chlorine, which can affect the fermentation process and the entire taste of the pickles. Distilled or filtered water is often recommended to ensure the purity and neutrality of the brine.

Spices and herbs are the artists' palette of the pickling world, allowing for endless creativity in flavoring pickled products. Common spices include mustard seeds, peppercorns, dill, cloves, and allspice, each adding its unique profile to the mix. Fresh herbs like dill, bay leaves, and tarragon can also be used to infuse the pickles with aromatic flavors. Garlic, onions, and chili peppers are popular additions for their ability to impart depth and heat.

Finally, the star ingredients of any pickling process are the fruits, vegetables, or even meats being preserved. The quality and freshness of these ingredients are paramount; they should be ripe but not overripe, free from bruises or blemishes, and thoroughly washed. The variety of produce that can be pickled is vast, from cucumbers, carrots, and beets to more unusual choices like watermelon rinds and green walnuts, offering a wide canvas for experimentation and enjoyment.

In conclusion, the equipment and ingredients needed for pickling are relatively simple but critical to the success of the preservation process. The right tools ensure cleanliness, safety, and precision, while the choice of ingredients—from the type of vinegar and spices to the quality of the produce—determines the flavor, texture, and nutritional value of the pickled goods. As individuals delve into the world of pickling, they join a long tradition of culinary preservation, enjoying not only the delicious results of their labor but also the satisfaction of mastering an age-old craft. With the basics in hand, the possibilities for creating unique and satisfying pickled products are nearly endless, inviting both novices and seasoned picklers to explore the depths of this versatile culinary art.

Various Pickling Methods (e.g., Vinegar, Salt, Brine)

A culinary skill that transforms fresh produce into preserved meals through the use of a variety of processes, pickling is a method that is rooted in tradition and has been practiced throughout civilizations for thousands of years. The capacity of pickling to extend the shelf life of perishable foods while simultaneously increasing their flavors and nutritional content is the quintessential characteristic of pickling. Several techniques are utilized in this process, which plays a significant role in the history of the evolution of human cuisine. Each of these techniques has its own set of traits and results. Vinegar pickling, salt pickling, and brine pickling are three of the most common and widely used pickling techniques. The purpose of this section is to investigate the many pickling techniques, elaborating on their processes, applications, and the distinctive flavors that they lend to the foods that they preserve.

The most common form of pickling is vinegar pickling, which includes drowning food in a solution of vinegar, water, salt, and frequently sugar, along with an array of spices for extra flavor. This method is likely the most widely used. Because it contains acetic acid, vinegar is a powerful preservative that works quickly to stop the growth of bacteria, so ensuring that the food will last for a longer period of time. This method is favored due to the fact that it is easy to use and may produce wonderful pickled foods in a short amount of time. Depending on the recipe, foods that are made using the vinegar pickling method are noted for having a tangy and sharp flavor that can range from sweet to sour with varying degrees of sweetness. Some of the vegetables that are typically pickled are cucumbers, onions, carrots, and beets. These vegetables are able to preserve their crisp texture while absorbing the flavors of the vinegar solution. The versatility of vinegar pickling, which enables a wide variety of flavor combinations to be achieved through the addition of spices like dill, mustard seed, and garlic, has made it a popular choice among both amateur cooks and professional producers.

The process of salt pickling is another time-honored method that use dry salt or a saltwater solution to extract moisture from the food. This process creates an environment that is unfriendly to the colonies of bacteria. This approach is frequently utilized for the preservation of vegetables, such as cabbage, in the preparation of sauerkraut or Korean kimchi. The salt not only helps to preserve the veggies, but it also kickstarts the fermentation process involving the vegetables. Due to the fact that the salt is able to extract water from the veggies, it creates a brine that promotes the growth of bacteria that produce lactic acid. The naturally occurring sugars in the veggies are fermented by these bacteria, which results in the production of lactic acid, which operates as a natural preservative. The end result is a product that is an abundant source of probiotics, has a distinct sour flavor, and has a texture that is crunchy. The health benefits of salt pickling are well-known and widely recognized. These benefits include enhanced immune function and improved digestion, as well as the remarkable capacity of salt pickling to produce complex flavors through the straightforward process of fermentation.

Pickling with brine is a hybrid technique that incorporates elements of both vinegar and salt pickling. Submerging the meal in a solution of saltwater, which typically includes vinegar and a variety of flavoring additives, is the method that is considered. In comparison to pickling with merely salt, brine pickling has a lower concentration of salt, which means that the brine pickling procedure is less drying to the food and allows for a more gradual and regulated fermentation process. The process of brine pickling is unique in that it allows for the fermentation of foods in a liquid medium. This allows for the creation of a more varied flavor profile, which is less acidic than items that have been pickled with vinegar but more robust than those that have been preserved with salt alone. It is standard practice to preserve foods such as pickles, olives, and particular cheeses using this method. These foods are able to reap the benefits of brine pickling, which can result in the development of subtle flavors and soft textures. The adaptability of this process, as well as the depth of flavor that it provides to a broad variety of dishes, makes it a favorite among culinary lovers who are interested in exploring the nuances of pickled delicacies.

Due to the fact that every pickling method has its own set of benefits and results in a different flavor profile, selecting the appropriate method is an essential aspect to take into consideration during the pickling process. Vinegar pickling is an excellent choice for individuals who are looking for instant enjoyment and a straightforward method of preparation because of its rapid turnaround time and intense flavors. The natural fermentation process, on the other hand, is the focus of salt pickling, which is appealing to individuals who are interested in the health advantages of foods that are high in probiotics as well as the varied flavors that are generated through fermentation. Individuals who are interested in experimenting with a wider variety of pickled products will find that brine pickling, which is a process that falls somewhere in the middle of these two methods, provides a harmonious combination of flavor and texture.

A comprehensive understanding of the components and procedures involved in the pickling process is necessary for mastering the art of pickling, regardless of the preferred method. When choosing a pickling process, it is important to take into consideration a number of factors, including the kind of food that is being pickled, the taste profile that is wanted, and the purpose for which the pickled product will be used. In addition, the act of pickling, which goes beyond the simple preservation of food, is a reflection of a cultural legacy and a culinary tradition that spans generations. It is a manifestation of the inventiveness and resourcefulness of cooks who, over the course of millennia, have learned to make use of the natural processes of fermentation and preservation in order to improve the nutrition of humans.

In conclusion, the several techniques of pickling, which range from brine to vinegar and salt, each make a distinctive contribution to the diverse array of cuisines that are found around the world. These techniques, which have their origins in the necessity of preservation, have developed into a culinary discipline that is lauded for its capacity to generate flavors and textures that are both gratifying to the tongue and nourishing to the body. Whether they are looking for the crisp tanginess of vinegar-pickled vegetables, the probiotic benefits of salt-fermented foods, or the complex flavors achieved through brine pickling, enthusiasts of this ancient art continue to explore and expand the boundaries of taste. In doing so, they preserve not only food, but also a time-honored tradition that strengthens our connection to the past and to one another.

CHAPTER III

The Science of Fermentation

Introduction to Fermentation

Fermentation is a fascinating and old biological process that has been mastered by humans for thousands of years. It serves not only as a means to preserve food but also to enhance the nutritional value and flavor of the food that is being preserved. This process, which is profoundly ingrained in the culinary traditions of a wide variety of cultures all over the world, involves the metabolic conversion of organic compounds by microbes and the enzymes that they produce. Bacteria and yeasts are the organisms that are responsible for the most frequent types of fermentation. These organisms convert sugars and starches into alcohol, carbon dioxide, and organic acids using fermentation. The purpose of this section is to provide an introduction to the art and science of fermentation. It will investigate the historical significance of fermentation, the fundamental principles that underlie the process, and the various uses of fermentation in the creation of food and beverages.

As indicated by archeological discoveries of fermented beverages and foods, fermentation is one of the oldest methods of food preservation. It dates back to the Neolithic period, making it one of the oldest methods. As humans searched for ways to extend the shelf life of perishable goods and discovered the pleasant aromas and textures that fermentation could generate, the practice most likely emerged independently in a number of different regions. The manufacture of beer in ancient

Mesopotamia and wine in Georgia, as well as the production of soy sauce in China and kimchi in Korea, are all examples of how fermentation has played an important part in human culture and nutrition. Not only did these early discoveries supply populations with reliable sources of food, but they also filled the cuisines of those groups with distinctive flavors that have been handed down from generation to generation.

The action of microorganisms of many kinds, including bacteria, yeasts, and molds, is at the center of the fundamental principles that underlie fermentation. The sugars that are found in food are consumed by these organisms, which then create other chemicals from those sugars. The fermentation of lactic acid, for instance, involves the transformation of carbohydrates into lactic acid by lactobacillus bacteria. Lactic acid serves as a natural preservative because it lowers the pH of the environment and creates a setting that is unfriendly to bacteria that are damaging to the organism. On the other hand, yeasts are responsible for the conversion of carbohydrates into ethanol and carbon dioxide during the process of alcohol fermentation. This is an essential step in the manufacturing of alcoholic beverages such as beer, wine, as well as spirits. Each form of fermentation is affected by a variety of elements, including temperature, pH, and the concentration of salt or sugar. These variables can be altered to encourage the growth of the microbes that are wanted and to generate particular flavors and textures.

In the production of food as well as beverages, fermentation plays a significant and multifaceted function. It is possible for fermentation to improve the nutritional composition of foods in addition to preserving them. Additionally, it decreases the amount of antinutrients and develops probiotics, both of which are important to the health of the gut. It also increases the availability of vitamins as well as minerals for absorption.

Because of this, fermented foods and beverages are highly regarded not only for the complexity of their flavors but also for the health benefits they offer, such as enhanced digestion and enhanced immune function.

The adaptability of the fermentation process is demonstrated by the wide variety of products that end up being fermented. Lactose is converted to lactic acid by bacteria during the fermentation process of milk, which results in the thickening of milk proteins and the addition of tangy tastes. Dairy products including yogurt and cheese are generated through this process. In the domain of vegetables, sauerkraut and kimchi are produced by fermenting cabbage with a variety of spices. This process results in condiments that are crispy, acidic, and rich in vitamins and probiotics. It is through the process of fermentation that grains and legumes are transformed into sourdough bread, tempeh, and miso. This demonstrates how fermentation can turn even the most basic components into foods that are both healthful and delectable.

In addition to its applications in the culinary world, fermentation is also significant from a cultural perspective. It is a living tradition that embodies the knowledge and traditions of predecessors, and it reflects a profound connection to the generations that came before us. A significant part of social rituals and festivities is frequently played by fermented foods and beverages, which serve as a symbol of the bountiful nature of the land and the continuous existence of the community. Furthermore, the resurgence of interest in classical fermentation techniques among contemporary chefs and home cooks is indicative of a growing respect for environmentally responsible food practices as well as a desire to acquire a more in-depth comprehension of the origins of food and the methodology behind its preparation.

Significant progress has been made in the field of fermentation science over the past few years, which has helped shed light on the intricate interactions that take place between bacteria and the substrates they consume. Because of this understanding, not only has the safety and consistency of fermented goods been enhanced, but it has also opened up new areas for innovation in the development of flavors and the optimization of health. In addition, the do-it-yourself movement has embraced fermentation as a means of reestablishing a connection with food. This has resulted in the encouragement of experimentation as well as the circulation of recipes and techniques among a thriving community of enthusiasts.

In conclusion, fermentation is a unique process that crosses the gap between science and art, as well as between tradition and creativity. Because of its capacity to preserve food, improve its flavor and nutritional content, and establish a connection between us and our cultural history, fermentation is an essential component of the human culinary experience. As we continue to investigate and obtain a better understanding of the complexities of fermentation, we not only pay homage to the inventiveness of our predecessors, but we also contribute to a future that is both sustainable and healthy. The products of fermentation enrich our meals and our lives with flavors that are as complex and diverse as the cultures from which they originate. This is true whether we are referring to the sour crunch of sauerkraut, the creamy richness of yogurt, or the refreshing effervescence of a glass of kombucha.

How Fermentation Works

The metabolic process known as fermentation is responsible for the transformation of sugar into acids, gases, or alcohol. Not only does it take place in yeast and bacteria, but it also takes place in muscle cells that are deficient in oxygen, as is the case with lactic acid fermentation. The science of fermentation is both complex and fascinating, involving a series of biochemical reactions that harness the power of microorganisms to transform food and beverages. This section delves into the intricate workings of fermentation, shedding light on the biochemical processes involved, the role of microorganisms, and the conditions necessary for fermentation to occur.

At its core, fermentation is an anaerobic process, meaning it does not require oxygen to proceed. This distinguishes it from aerobic respiration, where oxygen is taken as a reactant along with the organic fuel. In fermentation, microorganisms including yeast and bacteria play a pivotal role, acting as the catalysts that drive the transformation of substrates, such as glucose, into other chemical products. The most common products of fermentation are ethanol, carbon dioxide, and lactic acid, although the specific outcomes can vary widely depending on the type of microorganism involved and the conditions under which fermentation is carried out.

The process of fermentation begins with glycolysis, the breakdown of glucose. This initial step is universal to both aerobic respiration and anaerobic fermentation. The process of glycolysis involves the transformation of a single molecule of glucose producing two molecules of pyruvate, which results in the release of a little quantity of energy that was previously stored in adenosine triphosphate (ATP). It is possible for this process to take place in anaerobic settings since it takes place in the cytoplasm of the cell and doesn't need the oxygen presence.

Following glycolysis, the pathway of fermentation diverges from aerobic respiration. When there is no oxygen present, the pyruvate molecules produced during glycolysis undergo further transformation. In alcoholic fermentation, typically carried out by yeasts, pyruvate is converted onto ethanol and carbon dioxide. This conversion involves two key steps: first, the decarboxylation of pyruvate to produce acetaldehyde and carbon dioxide; and second, the reduction of acetaldehyde to ethanol, a reaction that also regenerates the coenzyme NAD+, allowing glycolysis to continue.

Lactic acid fermentation, on the other hand, involves the direct conversion of pyruvate into lactic acid. This process is carried out by certain bacteria, including the lactobacilli found in yogurt and the muscles cells during strenuous exercise. In this type of fermentation, the NADH produced during glycolysis is used to reduce pyruvate directly into lactic acid, once again regenerating NAD+ in the process. This regeneration is crucial as it enables glycolysis to proceed, ensuring a continuous supply of ATP in the absence of oxygen.

The environmental conditions under which fermentation occurs are vital to the process. Temperature, pH, and the concentration of salt and sugar can all influence the activity of fermenting microorganisms and the quality of the fermented product. Most microorganisms involved in fermentation thrive at specific temperatures and pH levels. For instance, the yeast used in brewing and winemaking performs optimally at temperatures between 20°C to 30°C, while lactic acid bacteria prefer slightly warmer conditions. Similarly, the acidity or alkalinity of the environment can affect the growth of microorganisms, with most fermentative bacteria favoring slightly acidic conditions.

The substrates used in fermentation, typically simple sugars like glucose, fructose, and sucrose, are another critical factor. The source of these sugars varies, from the maltose in barley malt used in beer production to the lactose in milk for yogurt and cheese. The type of sugar and its concentration can influence both the speed of fermentation and the types of products formed. In brewing, for example, higher sugar concentrations can lead to higher alcohol content, provided the yeast strain used can tolerate the resulting increase in alcohol.

Fermentation's end products are as diverse as the processes and conditions that create them. Ethanol and carbon dioxide are the hallmarks of alcoholic fermentation, giving us beer, wine, and spirits. Lactic acid is the key product of lactic acid fermentation, responsible for the sour taste of yogurt, sauerkraut, and sourdough bread. But beyond these, fermentation can also produce a plethora of other compounds, including vitamins, amino acids, and other organic acids, contributing to the nutritional value and complex flavors of fermented foods.

In conclusion, fermentation is a multifaceted biochemical process driven by the activity of microorganisms under anaerobic conditions. It transforms simple sugars into a variety of chemical products, depending on the type of microorganism involved and the specific conditions of fermentation. This process not only extends the shelf life of foods and beverages but also enhances their nutritional value and flavor profiles. Understanding how fermentation works provides valuable insights into this ancient practice, revealing the scientific principles that underpin one of humanity's oldest and most cherished culinary traditions. As we continue to explore and harness the power of fermentation, we unlock new possibilities for innovation in food and beverage production, ensuring that this time-honored process remains a vital part of our culinary heritage.

Different Types of Fermentation (e.g., Lactic Acid, Alcohol)

A metabolic process that has been exploited by humans for thousands of years, fermentation enables the preservation of food, the improvement of flavors, and the manufacture of alcohol. People have been using fermentation for thousands of years. In its most fundamental form, fermentation is characterized by the transformation of carbohydrates into alcohols and acids by the action of microorganisms in an anaerobic environment. There are multiple various forms of the process, each of which is distinguished by its own specific collection of biological reactions and end products. The process is not uniform; it comprises both types. Lactic acid fermentation and also alcoholic fermentation are two types of fermentation that are considered to be among the most significant and commonly used types of fermentation. This section examines the two basic types of fermentation, as well as other notable varieties, focusing on the methods, applications, and products that are produced by each type of fermentation.

A process known as lactic acid fermentation is responsible for the conversion of carbohydrates, more specifically glucose, lactose, and sucrose, into cellular energy as well as the metabolite lactate. Numerous types of bacteria, such as Lactobacillus, Streptococcus, and Leuconostoc, amongst others, are responsible for carrying out this particular form of fermentation. In the procedure of lactic acid fermentation, the sugar is initially converted into pyruvate through the physiological process known as glycolysis. Following this, the enzyme lactate dehydrogenase is responsible for the metabolic transformation of the pyruvate into lactate. This conversion is essential for the regeneration of NAD+, which is required for the continuation of glycolysis and for the cells to be able to generate energy in anaerobic conditions. Lactic acid fermentation is an essential step in the manufacturing process of a wide variety of food products, including sourdough bread, yogurt, sauerkraut, and kimchi, among others. Not only are these foods prized for the peculiar sour aromas they possess, but they are also appreciated for the health benefits they offer, which include the facilitation of digestion and the availability of probiotics.

The process of alcoholic fermentation, on the other hand, is predominantly linked with yeast, and more specifically with Saccharomyces cerevisiae. In this kind of fermentation, the breakdown of glucose by glycolysis results in the development of pyruvate, which is then transformed into ethanol and carbon dioxide. This conversion is comprised of two primary stages: the first stage is the decarboxylation of pyruvate to acetaldehyde, and the second stage is the reduction of acetaldehyde to ethanol respectively. The process of alcoholic fermentation is the foundation for the manufacturing of alcoholic beverages such as beer, wine, and spirits. This process makes use of the inherent capacity of yeast to convert sugars that are found in grains, fruits, and other sources into alcohol and carbon dioxide. During the fermentation process, carbon dioxide is generated, which is responsible for the characteristic bubbles that are found in beer and sparkling wines. On the other hand, ethanol is a contributor to the amount of alcohol that is present.

In addition to the fermentation of lactic acid and alcohol, there are a number of other notable types of fermentation that play important roles in the field of food science and business. For example, acetic acid fermentation is a two-step process that requires bacteria belonging to the species Acetobacter converting ethanol to acetic acid. This process is referred to as acetic acid fermentation. Vinegar is a standard in culinary practices all over the world, and it is used as both a condiment and a preservative. Vinegar is produced by a form of fermentation that is responsible for its manufacture. The acetic acid that is created during the fermentation process is directly responsible for the sharp and sour flavor that vinegar possesses.

The fermentation of butyric acid, which is carried out by particular species of Clostridium, is yet another significant type of fermentation. The carbohydrates fermentation results in the production of butyric acid, along with trace amounts of acetone and isopropanol. This process is an example of a fermentation. The strong and frequently unpleasant odor of butyric acid is one of the reasons why fermentation of butyric acid is not as common in the food production industry. The fact that it plays a part in the production of some traditional foods, such as certain kinds of cheese, and that it has applications in industrial biotechnology are both intriguing aspects of this substance.

Another type of fermentation is called propionic acid fermentation, and it is primarily carried out by Propionibacterium species. This type of fermentation converts lactate into propionic acid, acetic acid, and carbon dioxide. In the process of making Swiss cheese, this particular type of fermentation is essential since it is the carbon dioxide that creates the holes that are characteristic of Swiss cheese, and the propionic acid that contributes to the cheese's distinctive flavor.

The individual microorganisms that are involved in each kind of fermentation, the substrates that they metabolize, and the ambient circumstances that favor their activity are what differentiate each type of fermentation from the others. In order to maximize the effectiveness of the fermentation process and produce the products that are wanted, it is necessary to exercise strict control over the temperature, pH, and anaerobic conditions. Furthermore, the selection of microorganisms and the composition of the medium used for fermentation can have a substantial impact on the flavor, texture, and nutritional qualities of the food that has been fermented.

Fermentation processes are extremely versatile, which highlights their significance in a wide variety of applications. These applications include the manufacture of food and beverages, pharmaceuticals, and biofuels, among others. Not only have humans been able to preserve foods through the process of fermentation, but they have also been able to generate a wide variety of novel flavors and sensations, which has contributed to the expansion of our palette. There are many examples that demonstrate the diversity and relevance of fermentation in our diet and culture. Some examples include the manufacture of alcoholic beverages, the tangy flavor of fermented dairy and vegetables, and the distinctive flavors of fermented grains and legumes.

In conclusion, fermentation is a group of processes that are both complicated and diverse. These processes utilize the metabolic activity of microbes to convert carbohydrates into alcohols, acids, and gases. The fermentation of lactic acid and alcoholic beverages are two of the most common and culturally significant types of fermentation. These fermentations are responsible for the manufacture of an array of food and beverage products that are essential to the diets of people all over the world. We are able to grasp the depth and breadth of this ancient science when we have a solid understanding of the various forms of fermentation, the biochemical foundations upon which they are based, and the uses of these fermentations. By continuing to investigate the possibilities of fermentation, we are able to unleash fresh potential for innovation in the fields of food science, nutrition, and other areas. In doing so, we are commemorating a tradition that has been an essential component of human civilization for over a thousand years.

Key Ingredients and Tools for Fermentation

Fermentation is a transformative process that has been a cornerstone of culinary traditions across the globe for thousands of years. This biological phenomenon, harnessed by humans for the preservation of food and the enhancement of flavors, requires specific ingredients and tools to catalyze the conversion of sugars into alcohol, acids, and/or gases. The art and science of fermentation are underpinned by these essential components, each playing a pivotal role in the successful creation of fermented products. This section delves into the key ingredients and tools necessary for fermentation, highlighting how they contribute to the process and the variety of products that can be achieved.

At the heart of any fermentation process are the microorganisms, such as yeast and bacteria, that drive the transformation. Yeast, particularly Saccharomyces cerevisiae, is instrumental in alcoholic fermentation, converting sugars into ethanol and also carbon dioxide. This microorganism is a critical ingredient in the production of beer, wine, and bread. Bacteria play a central role in lactic acid fermentation, with species like Lactobacillus transforming sugars into lactic acid, a preservative that imparts a tangy flavor to products such as yogurt, sauerkraut, and kimchi. The selection of the right strain of yeast or bacteria is crucial, as it determines the flavor, texture, and nutritional profile of the fermented product.

Sugars are the fuel for fermentation, serving as the primary substrate that microorganisms metabolize. The source of these sugars varies widely, from the maltose in malted barley used in beer brewing to the lactose in milk for dairy fermentation. The type of sugar and its concentration can significantly influence the fermentation process, affecting the rate of fermentation and the characteristics of the finished product. In some cases, additional sugars are added to the fermentation medium to boost the activity of the microorganisms and achieve a desired level of alcohol or acidity.

Salts, particularly in lactic acid fermentation, play a dual role as flavor enhancers and preservatives. They create an environment that favors the growth of beneficial bacteria while inhibiting harmful ones. The concentration of salt can vary, based on the desired outcome, but must be carefully managed to ensure a successful fermentation process. In the making of kimchi and sauerkraut, for example, salt not only seasons the vegetables but also draws out water, creating a brine that facilitates the fermentation.

Water is the medium in which fermentation often occurs, dissolving salts, sugars, and other soluble ingredients to create a suitable environment for the microorganisms. The quality of water is important; it should be free from chlorine and other chemicals that can inhibit fermentation. In many fermentation processes, the water-to-soluble ingredient ratio is critical and must be precisely controlled to obtain the desired consistency and flavor of the fermented product.

Beyond these ingredients, the tools and equipment used in fermentation are equally important. Glass jars, ceramic crocks, and wooden barrels are common containers that provide an anaerobic environment necessary for fermentation to occur. These vessels should be non-reactive to ensure that they do not impart undesirable flavors to the product or interact chemically with the acidic contents. The choice of container often depends on the scale of fermentation and the specific product being made.

Airlocks and weights are tools specifically designed for fermentation, particularly for vegetables and other solid substrates. Airlocks allow carbon dioxide produced during fermentation to escape while preventing outside air, and potentially harmful microorganisms, from entering the container. Weights are used to keep the fermenting material submerged in its brine or liquid, ensuring an even and consistent fermentation process by preventing exposure to air that could lead to spoilage.

Thermometers and pH meters are critical for monitoring the fermentation environment. Temperature and pH can significantly affect the activity of fermenting microorganisms; too high or too low temperatures can inhibit fermentation or lead to the growth of undesirable bacteria. Similarly, an optimal pH range is essential for the successful fermentation of specific products. Monitoring and adjusting these parameters ensures a controlled fermentation process and a high-quality end product.

In conclusion, fermentation is a delicate balance of science and art, requiring specific ingredients and tools to guide the process to its delicious outcomes. Microorganisms, sugars, salts, and water interact under the careful watch of the fermenter, who uses containers, airlocks, weights, thermometers, and pH meters to create the perfect conditions for fermentation. The mastery of these elements opens up a world of culinary possibilities, allowing for the preservation of food, the enhancement of flavors, and the creation of an array of fermented products that have nourished and delighted humanity for centuries. As we explore and innovate within the realm of fermentation, the fundamental importance of these key ingredients and tools remains a constant guide, ensuring the legacy of fermentation continues to enrich our diets and cultures.

CHAPTER IV

Getting Started with Pickling

Selecting the Right Produce

Pickling is known as an ancient method of food preservation that has been done for thousands of years across a wide variety of civilizations for the purpose of preserving food. Not only does this culinary technique, which involves preserving food in an acidic solution or through fermentation, lengthen the shelf life of perishable foods, but it also enhances the flavor of these items and increases their nutritional content. The meticulous selection of produce is not only an essential stage in the pickling process, but it is also significant role in determining the overall quality and flavor of the products that are produced. This section examines the significance of selecting the appropriate produce for pickling, the elements that should be taken into consideration throughout the selection process, and the influence that the quality of the produce has on the pickling process.

It is of the utmost importance to choose the appropriate produce for pickling. Choosing fruits and vegetables that are both fresh and of good quality is the first step in the procedure. Because the state of the produce at the time of pickling has a significant impact on the texture, flavor, as well as the overall quality of the pickled product, freshness is of the utmost importance. Ideally, the best time to harvest produce is when it is at its pinnacle of maturity, when it is both the most flavorful and the most nutritious. Pickled vegetables that are overripe may result in mushy pickles, while pickled vegetables that are underripe may not develop the flavors that are desired throughout the pickling process.

In addition, quality is of equal measure. When choosing produce for pickling, it is important to make sure that it is devoid of any blemishes, bruises, or symptoms of deterioration. Not only can these flaws diminish the aesthetic attractiveness of pickled foods, but they also have the potential to influence their flavor and the length of time they can be stored. Microorganisms that could potentially interfere with the fermentation process or cause the pickle to become spoiled can be found in places that have been damaged or decaying. Therefore, in order to guarantee that the pickling endeavor will be successful, it is necessary to go through the processes of carefully inspecting and selecting the produce.

The dimensions and contours of the produce are still another essential aspect to take into consideration. Having parts that are the same size and shape ensures that they will pickle at the same rate, which ultimately results in a product that is consistent. It is especially crucial to keep this in mind when it comes to pickling vegetables like cucumbers, carrots, and green beans, which are typically pickled in large chunks or complete shapes. Furthermore, the process of cutting the produce into consistent pieces helps improve the penetration of the brine or vinegar, which in turn ensures that the tastes are dispersed evenly throughout the pickle.

The pickling procedure is also heavily influenced by the sort of product that is chosen to generate the pickled food. While pickling can be done with an array of fruits and vegetables, there are some that are more suited to the process than others. Cucumbers, for instance, are a traditional pickling ingredient because of their hard consistency and mild flavor, which allows them to readily absorb the flavors of the brine or vinegar that is used in the process. The vegetables carrots, beets, cabbage, and cauliflower are also among the most popular options. When it comes to picking fruits for pickling, selections such as cherries, pears, and peaches are preferred because of their capacity to keep their texture and flavor intact in the acidic environment of pickling.

An additional factor to take into account is the natural pH of the produce. It is possible for the pickling process to be influenced by the acidity or alkalinity of the food, particularly in fermentation, where the pH level can have an effect on the growth of bacteria that are advantageous to the process. Produce that has a lower natural pH (one that is more acidic) is typically more resistant to deterioration and can result in a pickled product that is more stable and tasty.

In addition, the amount of water that is present in the produce can have an effect on the pickling process. Vegetables with a high water content, such as cucumbers and radishes, have the potential to become excessively tender if they are not properly prepped before being pickled. It is possible to tackle this issue by employing techniques such as salting or pre-soaking the veggies in ice water. These techniques extract excess moisture from the vegetables and ensure that they retain their crunch after the pickling process.

Another aspect that should be taken into consideration is the origin of the produce. The use of seasonal produce that is produced locally not only helps to promote environmentally responsible agriculture practices, but it also guarantees that the fruits and vegetables are at their most tasty and freshest for consumption. Additionally, organic food, which is free of pesticides and other chemicals, can be a better alternative for pickling. This ensures that the finished result is as natural and wholesome as it can possibly be.

In conclusion, one of the most important aspects of successful pickling is the selection of food items that are suitable for pickling. The outcome of the pickling process is heavily influenced by a number of factors, including the freshness, quality, size, shape, kind, natural pH, and water content of the fruits and vegetables, as well as the source of the produce. It is possible for folks to improve the flavor, texture, and nutritional content of their pickled goods by giving careful consideration to the aforementioned elements. This will not only ensure that these preserved items stay longer but also that they taste better at the same time. As the interest in pickling continues to develop, both among culinary experts and home chefs, the careful selection of produce continues to be an essential stage in the process of generating pickled items that are of high quality, tasty, and nutritious, and that can be enjoyed for a number of months to come.

Preparing Vegetables and Fruits for Pickling

An art form that blends the science of food preservation with the art of pickling vegetables and fruits is the preparation of pickled vegetables and fruits. Using this method, fresh food is transformed into delectable pleasures that can be enjoyed throughout the year. This procedure captures the spirit of seasonal bounty and allows it to be enjoyed throughout the year. The route from fresh fruit to pickled perfection comprises a number of essential procedures, including selection, cleaning, cutting, brining, and seasoning. In order to guarantee the quality, safety, and flavor of the pickled products, each stage is considered to be equally important. This section goes into the intricate process of preparing fruits and vegetables for pickling, underlining the significance of each stage as well as the best practices that should be adhered to.

First and foremost, the pickling procedure begins with the careful selection of the fruit to be preserved. Pickling should only be done with pickled fruits and vegetables that are of the best quality and freshest possible. This involves choosing foods that are ripe but not overripe, free of bruises, blemishes, or symptoms of decomposition, and that are just right for consumption. When it comes to the finished product, freshness is extremely important because it has a direct influence on the texture, flavor, and overall quality of products. Pickling food that is overripe may result in a mushy texture after the pickling process, whereas pickling produce that is underripe may not absorb the pickling brine as efficiently.

It is vital to perform a thorough cleaning after the appropriate produce has been chosen. By performing this procedure, any dirt, bacteria, and residues that may be present on the surface of the fruits and vegetables are eliminated. The vegetables can be cleaned by rinsing it under cold running water or by using a vegetable brush for foods with more difficult skins. Both of these methods are effective. Vinegar and water can be combined together to create a solution that can be used to thoroughly clean organic fruit or other objects that have skins that can be eaten. For the purpose of preventing the entrance of undesirable bacteria into the pickling jar, which could potentially cause the batch to go bad, this rigorous cleaning is absolutely necessary.

The following step entails slicing the fruit into the proper shapes and sizes of the finished product. This may involve slicing cucumbers into spears or rounds, chopping beets into cubes, or leaving small fruits like cherries in their complete form. It is essential to maintain consistency in this situation; making sure that all of the pieces are of the same size will promote even pickling and texture. Furthermore, the manner in which the produce is chopped might have an effect on the penetration of the pickling solution, which in turn can have an effect on the flavor and firmness of the final result. When it comes to certain kinds of vegetables, such as cucumbers and zucchinis, which contain a lot of water, pre-salting or utilizing an ice-water bath can help take out moisture, which will prevent the pickles from getting overly wet.

In the process of pickling, brining is an additional preparatory step that is of critical importance. In most cases, the brine, which is often a combination of water, vinegar, salt, and occasionally sugar, serves as the medium for pickling. The concentration of salt and vinegar in the brine is quite important; it must be high enough to prevent the growth of germs that are detrimental to the organisms while still allowing the fermentation process to take place as desired, particularly in the case of pickles that are fermented using lactose. Although the specific gravity or salinity of the brine might change based on the recipe and the kind of fruit that is being pickled, it is absolutely necessary in order to guarantee the safety of the pickled goods and to ensure that they will last for a long time.

One of the most important aspects of the pickling process is the seasoning of the brine. This process involves the incorporation of aromatics, herbs, and spices into the produce in order to impart some of their flavors. Dill, garlic, mustard seeds, peppercorns, bay leaves, and other popular flavors are only some of the ingredients that are commonly used. There is a large range of seasonings available, which enables an infinite amount of creativity to be expressed in pickling recipes. Before the jar is sealed, the seasonings are often added to the brine or straight to the containers themselves. Some of these spices, such as cinnamon or cloves, have the potential to become overbearing if they are used in excessive amounts. It is essential to take this into consideration.

The packing of the vegetables into pickling jars is the final step in the preparation process that comes before the actual pickling process. One must proceed with caution in order to guarantee that the fruits or vegetables are completely buried in the brine, while also ensuring that there is sufficient headroom in the jar to accommodate the expansion of the brine. For the purpose of maintaining an anaerobic environment that is conducive to the fermentation process, the utilization of weights or followers can be of great assistance in maintaining the submersion of the produce, particularly in the context of fermentation-based pickling.

In conclusion, the process of preparing fruits and vegetables for pickling is a lengthy and laborious one that necessitates careful attention to detail at each and every stage. The safety, quality, and flavor of the pickled items are all dependent on the several steps that are taken, beginning with the selection of the freshest fruit and continuing through cleaning, chopping, brining, and seasoning. By adhering to best standards in preparation, picklers are able to create pickled goods that are not only delicious but also safe, showcasing the tastes of the produce as well as the pickler's artistic ability. In order to master the trade of pickling, it is vital to understand and respect the process of preparation. This is true regardless of whether one is an experienced pickler or a novice. This will ensure that the tradition of preserving the bounty of the seasons can continue to be enjoyed by future generations.

Basic Pickling Recipes and Techniques

Pickling is known as a time-honored method of food preservation that has been embraced by cultures all over the world due to its capacity to increase the shelf life of perishable goods while simultaneously improving its flavor and nutritional content. For the purpose of preventing the spoiling of fruits, vegetables, and even meats, this culinary technique includes submerging them in an acidic solution or fermenting them. The fundamental methods and recipes for pickling are varied, ranging from straightforward pickles made with vinegar to intricate fermented concoctions created by fermentation. Within the scope of this section, the fundamental recipes and techniques of pickling are investigated, providing insights into the art and science that lie behind this time-honored custom.

The most important aspect of pickling is the creation of an acidic environment for the purpose of preserving the food. This can be accomplished by adding vinegar to the mixture or by utilizing natural fermentation processes such as fermentation. Vinegar-based pickling, sometimes referred to as quick pickling, is the procedure that is both the easiest and the quickest to implement. Creating a pickling brine is accomplished by the use of this method, which entails combining water and vinegar, frequently with salt and sugar. The acidity of the vinegar hinders the development of bacteria which cause the food to go bad, which successfully preserves the food. To enhance the flavor of this basic brine, an array of spices and herbs, including dill, mustard seeds, garlic, and peppercorns, can be added. After being submerged in the brine, the food, which may include cucumbers for traditional dill pickles or carrots and radishes for a mixed vegetable pickle, is then stored in containers that are airtight. Home cooks who are trying to add a sour crunch to their dishes will find that quick pickles are a convenient alternative because they can be consumed within hours or days of being prepared.

Pickling that is based on fermentation is a process that depends on the natural lacto-fermentation of vegetables and takes more time than other pickling methods. Utilizing salt, either in the form of a dry rub or a brine solution, this technique is utilized to extract moisture from the produce and to establish an atmosphere that is favorable to the development of lactic acid bacteria that are advantageous to the process. In order to produce lactic acid, which functions as a natural preservative, these bacteria consume the natural sugars that are present in the food and convert them into lactic acid. Examples of fermented pickles that are considered to be classics are sauerkraut, which is produced from cabbage, and kimchi, which is a Korean delicacy that is made using a combination of vegetables and flavors. Not only are fermented pickles renowned for their complexity of flavor, but they are also highly regarded for the probiotic health advantages they offer, which help to maintain a healthy microbiota in the stomach.

The recipe for the traditional cucumber dill pickle is widely considered to be one of the most fundamental and well-liked pickling recipes. In order to prepare this, cucumbers are first washed and sliced to the correct size. Next, they are packed into jars together with fresh dill, garlic cloves, and maybe a dusting of red pepper flakes for added spice. After bringing to a boil a brine that is composed of water and vinegar in equal proportions, seasoned with salt and a touch of sugar, the brine is then poured over the cucumbers, thoroughly coating them. In order to prepare the jars for storage in the refrigerator, they are first sealed and then allowed to cool. Pickled cucumbers are ready to be consumed as a snack or as an addition to meals after a few days have passed. They are crisp and tasty, and they are ready to be savored.

An additional fundamental dish that demonstrates the process of fermentation is the preparation of sauerkraut at home. The first step in this process involves slicing the cabbage very thinly and then rubbing it with salt until it releases its pure juices. The cabbage that has been salted is then packed snugly into a jar that has been thoroughly cleaned, making sure that it is completely buried in the liquid. This is accomplished by placing a weight on top of the jar to ensure that the cabbage remains immersed, and then covering the jar with a cloth to enable gasses to escape while preventing pollutants from entering. During the fermentation process, which can take anywhere from a few days to a few weeks and takes place at room temperature, the cabbage develops a flavor that is tart and a texture that is soft yet crunchy. The end product is a sauerkraut that is loaded with probiotics and may be consumed on its own or as a tasty element that can be added to a wide range of recipes.

A mixed vegetable pickle presents a wonderful chance for individuals who are interested in broadening their knowledge of the diverse applications of vinegar-based pickling beyond the realm of cucumbers. It is possible to combine aromatic spices like coriander, cumin, and turmeric with bite-sized pieces of vegetables like carrots, green beans, cauliflower, and peppers. Additionally, these vegetables can be sliced into bite-sized pieces. Following that, the vegetables are marinated in a hot vinegar brine, which is quite similar to the process for cucumber pickles, and then they are let to sit. As a result of the spices infusing the veggies with robust tastes, the pickle that is produced is visually pleasing as well as gastronomically intriguing.

Pickling recipes and procedures that are considered to be fundamental offer home cooks a foundation upon which they can explore and grow their pickling repertoire. The key to good pickling rests in having an awareness of the principles that govern the preservation process. This is true whether one chooses to go with the basic and speedy method of vinegar-based pickling or to delve into the slow art of fermentation. Cooks are able to make a wide variety of pickled treats that are a celebration of the wealth that the seasons provide by selecting fresh, high-quality fruit, meticulously preparing the brine or fermentation medium, and experimenting with different flavors.

Pickling stands out as a culinary discipline that is both adaptable and gratifying, allowing unlimited possibilities for creativity and flavor exploration. Because of this, pickling is becoming increasingly popular as the interest in ancient ways of food preservation continues to develop.

Troubleshooting Common Pickling Problems

The process of pickling, which involves preserving food by means of fermentation or immersion in an acidic liquid, is a procedure that is entrenched in history and is blessed with a wealth of tradition. Despite the fact that the technique has the potential to enhance the flavor of fruits and vegetables and extend their shelf life, it also has the potential to provide a variety of obstacles, even for the most expert picklers. The final product's quality can be negatively impacted by a variety of common issues, including cloudiness in the brine, pickles that are soft or mushy, and flavors that are not to the consumer's liking. In order to guarantee successful pickling results, it is essential to have a solid understanding of how to troubleshoot certain problems. The answers to these typical pickling difficulties are investigated in this section, which also provides insights into the sources of these problems and recommendations for remedial measures that can be performed to remedy them.

One of the most common problems that arises during the process of pickling is cloudiness in the brine. This cloudiness can be brought on by a number of different circumstances, such as the utilization of tap water that is rich in minerals, the presence of bacteria as a result of faulty sterilization, or the breakdown of the product that is being pickled. To avoid this, it is recommended that you use water that has been distilled or filtered, as these types of water do not include any minerals that could potentially react with the pickling process. An additional measure that may be taken to reduce the likelihood of bacterial contamination is to make certain that all of the jars and equipment are fully cleaned and sterilized before being used. When using cucumbers or other vegetables of a similar nature, it is recommended that the bloom end be removed. This is because the flower end contains enzymes that might produce cloudiness.

The formation of pickles that are soft or mushy is another common concern. This is a letdown for people who love their pickles to be crisp and crunchy whenever they consume them. This problem is frequently caused by the natural enzymes that are present in the veggies, which continue to degrade the cellular walls even when the vegetables are being pickled. One strategy that can be used to solve this issue is to soak the vegetables in ice water for a number of hours prior to pickling them. This can assist in making the vegetables more consistent. Furthermore, the addition of grape, oak, or horseradish leaves to the pickling jar might bring tannins, which contribute to the preservation of the crunchiness of the pickled ingredient. In addition, it is possible to maintain the proper texture by ensuring that the brine is at the appropriate temperature when it is poured over the vegetables and by avoiding overprocessing the jars in a water bath without exceeding the temperature.

When it comes to pickled items, off-flavors can be especially discouraging because they have the potential to render the fruits of one's labor intoxicating. It is possible for these flavors to originate from a variety of sources, such as germs that cause decomposition, the utilization of spices that are either outdated or of low quality, or contamination from metallic tools or containers. For the purpose of avoiding these problems, it is essential to make use of only fresh spices of the highest possible quality and to make certain that all containers and utensils are constructed from non-reactive materials such as glass, stainless steel, or plastic that is fit for food. In addition, ensuring that the brine contains the appropriate proportions of vinegar, water, and salt in accordance with the recipes that have been tried and tested will assist in preventing the growth of perishable bacteria that can result in unpleasant flavors.

One further difficulty that may occur is the inability of the pickling process to begin, which is especially problematic in the case of fermented pickles. It is possible that this failure was caused by a number of different circumstances, such as an inadequate concentration of salt, temperatures that are too low for fermentation to take place, or the utilization of produce that has been treated with chemicals that impede the growth of bacteria. In order to handle this issue, it is vital to make certain that the salt concentration level is sufficient and falls within the range that is advised for fermentation. It is also possible to encourage the activity of the beneficial bacteria that are responsible for fermentation by maintaining the fermenting produce at a temperature that falls between 55 and 75 degrees Fahrenheit. By carefully washing the produce or by using organic food, one can reduce the likelihood of chemical residues that could potentially interfere with the fermentation process.

Lastly, the presence of mold on the surface of fermented pickles is something that may offer cause for concern. The presence of colored molds is an indication that the batch has gone bad, and it is recommended that the affected batch be thrown away. A little amount of white yeast, often known as "kahm yeast," is common and does not pose any health risks. It is essential to keep the veggies immersed below the surface of the brine in order to prevent the growth of mold. This is because mold can be encouraged to flourish when it is exposed to outside air. Helping to maintain an anaerobic atmosphere that is suitable to safe fermentation can be accomplished by the utilization of a clean weight or a fermentation cover that is designed to release gases while keeping air from entering.

In conclusion, pickling is a culinary undertaking that is not without its problems, despite the fact that it is simultaneously gratifying and fun. There are a number of typical problems that can have a negative effect on the quality of pickled products. These problems include cloudiness in the brine, pickles that are soft or mushy, lack of flavor, failure to ferment, and the growth of mold. On the other hand, picklers can significantly improve their chances of success by first gaining an understanding of the factors that contribute to these issues and then taking the appropriate corrective actions. These include the utilization of distilled water, the guarantee of proper sterilization, the addition of tannin-rich leaves, the maintenance of the appropriate brine balance, and the establishment of an anaerobic environment. Through the use of patience, practice, and careful attention to detail, the art of pickling can produce results that are both delectable and rewarding. This will ensure that the age- old custom of preserving the bounty of the seasons will be carried on for all future generations.

Chapter V

Exploring Fermentation Techniques

Fermenting Vegetables

Fermenting vegetables is an ancient culinary practice that has surged in popularity in recent years, due to its health benefits and the global revival of traditional food preservation techniques. This method of preservation, which relies on the process of lacto-fermentation, not only extends the shelf life of fresh produce but also enhances its nutritional value and flavor profile. The essence of vegetable fermentation lies in creating conditions that favor the growth of beneficial lactic acid bacteria, transforming the natural sugars in vegetables into lactic acid. This section delves into the fundamentals of fermenting vegetables, covering the science behind the process, the health benefits, the variety of vegetables that can be fermented, and some basic techniques and tips for successful fermentation.

At the heart of vegetable fermentation is lacto-fermentation, a metabolic process performed by certain strains of lactic acid bacteria, predominantly from the genus Lactobacillus. These bacteria are naturally present on the surface of all plants, especially those grown close to the ground. The fermentation process begins when vegetables are submerged in a brine solution or their juices, creating an anaerobic (oxygen-free) environment. Salt, added to the brine, plays a crucial role by inhibiting the development of harmful bacteria and fungi while promoting the proliferation of lactic acid bacteria. As these beneficial bacteria consume the sugars present in the vegetables, they generate lactic acid, which acts as a natural preservative, lowering the pH of the environment and preventing spoilage.

The health benefits of fermented vegetables are numerous. The fermentation process not only preserves the vegetables but also makes them more digestible and increases the bioavailability of nutrients, making it simpler for the body to absorb the vitamins and minerals they contain. Fermented vegetables are known as a rich source of probiotics, live microorganisms that participate to a healthy gut microbiome, which is connected to improved digestion, enhanced immune function, and minimized risk of some chronic diseases. The fermentation process can also produce new nutrients, including B vitamins and beneficial enzymes.

Various vegetables can be successfully fermented, offering a palette of flavors and textures. Commonly fermented vegetables include cabbage (transformed into sauerkraut or kimchi), cucumbers (to make pickles), carrots, beets, radishes, and cauliflower. However, the possibilities are nearly endless, allowing for creativity and experimentation in the kitchen. Each type of vegetable brings its unique taste and nutritional profile to the fermentation process, and adding herbs, spices, and other flavorings can further enhance the complexity of the final product.

The basic technique for fermenting vegetables involves preparing the vegetables (washing, peeling, chopping, or slicing), mixing them with salt to draw out moisture and create a brine, and then packing them tightly into clean jars. The vegetables must be fully submerged in the brine to prevent exposure to air, which could lead to mold or yeast growth. A weight is often used to keep the vegetables below the brine's surface, and a cloth or fermentation lid can cover the jar to allow gases produced during the fermentation to escape while keeping contaminants out. The jars are then stored at room temperature, away from direct sunlight, for a period ranging from a few days to several weeks, depending on the desired level of fermentation and the ambient temperature.

Throughout the fermentation process, it's essential to monitor the vegetables for signs of successful fermentation, such as the presence of bubbles, a tangy aroma, and a pleasant, sour taste. It's also important to be vigilant for any signs of spoilage, such as off-odors, mold, or a slimy texture, which indicate that the batch should be discarded. Proper equipment sanitation, using the correct salt concentration (typically 2-5% by weight), and maintaining an anaerobic environment are critical factors in ensuring the success and safety of vegetable fermentation.

In conclusion, fermenting vegetables is a rewarding endeavor that connects us to our culinary heritage while offering significant health benefits. The process of lacto-fermentation transforms ordinary vegetables into probiotic-rich superfoods, enhancing their flavor and nutritional content. With a basic understanding of the science behind fermentation, the right techniques, and a bit of patience, anyone can master the art of fermenting vegetables. Whether it's the crisp tanginess of sauerkraut, the spicy complexity of kimchi, or the refreshing bite of pickled cucumbers, fermented vegetables offer a delicious and healthful addition to any meal, showcasing the timeless wisdom of traditional food preservation methods.

Fermenting Fruits

Fermenting fruits, an ancient practice that dates back centuries, offers a fascinating intersection of culture, culinary art, and microbiology. This process, akin to vegetable fermentation, involves the transformation of fruits using beneficial bacteria, yeasts, and sometimes molds, to produce various flavorful and healthful products. Fermented fruits can range from mildly tangy to distinctly sour or even alcoholic, depending on the specific fermentation process employed. This section explores the process of fermenting fruits, including the science behind it, the health benefits, the types of fruits that can be fermented, and the various culinary uses of fermented fruit products.

The science of fermenting fruits is based on the natural occurrence of microorganisms including yeast and bacteria on the skin of fruits. When fruits are submerged in an anaerobic (oxygen-free) environment, or their own juices, these microorganisms begin to metabolize the natural sugars present in the fruit, converting them into alcohol, carbon dioxide, and organic acids, particularly lactic and acetic acid. This process not only preserves the fruit but also creates complex flavors and aromas that are not present in the fresh fruit. The key to successful fruit fermentation is managing the microbial environment to encourage the growth of desirable microorganisms while inhibiting harmful ones. This is often achieved through the addition of salt or sugar, controlling temperature, and ensuring an anaerobic environment.

Fermented fruits offer numerous health benefits, primarily due to the presence of probiotics, the beneficial bacteria that support gut health. These microorganisms can help balance the gut microbiome, improving digestion and potentially enhancing immune function. Furthermore, the fruit's increased bioavailability due to fermentation helps facilitate the body's absorption of vital vitamins and minerals. Antioxidants—compounds that assist in counteracting damaging free radicals in the body and may lower the risk of chronic diseases—are also present in fermented fruits.

Various fruits can be fermented, each offering unique flavors and textures to explore. Commonly fermented fruits include apples, pears, plums, cherries, and berries. Tropical fruits like pineapples, mangoes, and papayas are also excellent candidates for fermentation, offering bold and exotic flavors. The choice of fruit often depends on personal preference and the desired end product, whether it's a tangy condiment, a refreshing beverage, or a complex alcoholic drink. When selecting fruits for fermentation, it's important to use ripe, high-quality produce free from bruises and blemishes to ensure the best flavor and nutritional value.

The culinary applications of fermented fruits are diverse and exciting. Fermented fruit chutneys and relishes can add a tangy contrast to rich dishes, while fermented fruit beverages, both alcoholic and non-alcoholic, offer refreshing and complex drink options. For example, kombucha, a popular fermented tea beverage, can be flavored with various fruits to create unique and healthful drinks. Additionally, fermented fruits can be used in baking and cooking, adding depth and acidity to sweets and savories alike. The fermentation of fruits can also lead to the production of vinegars, which are valuable both as culinary ingredients and for their health-promoting properties.

The process of fermenting fruits typically involves preparing the fruit by washing and cutting it into pieces, if necessary, and then submerging it in a brine solution or mixing it with sugar to draw out the juices. The addition of a starter culture, such as a SCOBY, also referred to as Symbiotic Culture Of Bacteria and Yeast, in the case of kombucha, or natural whey, can help kickstart the fermentation process, although it's not always necessary due to the natural presence of microorganisms on the skin of the fruit. The fruit mixture is then covered and left to ferment at room temperature for a period varying from a few days to several weeks, depending on the desired level of fermentation and the ambient conditions.

Throughout the fermentation process, it's essential to monitor the fruit for signs of successful fermentation, such as the production of bubbles and a pleasant, tangy aroma. It's also important to be vigilant for any spoilage, such as off-odors or mold, indicating that the batch should be discarded. Proper sanitation, the use of the correct concentration of salt or sugar, and maintaining an anaerobic environment are critical factors in ensuring the success and safety of fruit fermentation.

In conclusion, fermenting fruits is a rewarding practice that connects us to ancient traditions while offering a way to explore new flavors and reap health benefits. The process transforms simple fruits into probiotic-rich, flavorful, and nutritious products that can enhance a wide range of culinary creations. Whether enjoyed as a condiment, beverage, or ingredient, fermented fruits exemplify the incredible potential of fermentation to preserve and elevate our food. With patience, care, as well as a bit of experimentation, the art of fermenting fruits opens up a world of culinary possibilities, letting us to savor the tastes and benefits of this fascinating process.

Fermenting Dairy Products

Fermenting dairy products is a practice as ancient as agriculture itself, a cornerstone of culinary traditions across the globe. This process, which transforms milk into a variety of products such as yogurt, cheese, kefir, and buttermilk, is revered not only for its ability to preserve dairy but also for enhancing nutritional value, digestibility, and flavor. Dairy fermentation involves specific microorganisms that metabolize lactose, milk's sugar, into lactic acid, fundamentally altering the milk's properties. This section explores the intricacies of fermenting dairy products, delving into the science behind the process, the health benefits, the diversity of fermented dairy products, and the techniques employed in their production.

The science of dairy fermentation hinges on the metabolic activities of lactic acid bacteria (LAB), primarily Lactobacillus, Streptococcus, and Bifidobacterium species. These bacteria are remarkable for their ability to thrive in milk, a nutrient-rich environment, where they convert lactose into lactic acid. This acidification procedure lowers the pH of the milk, causing proteins, mainly casein, to coagulate and form the basis of many fermented dairy products. The extent of fermentation, controlled by factors such as the strain of bacteria, temperature, and fermentation time, determines the final product's texture, taste, and nutritional profile.

The health benefits of fermented dairy are manifold. The fermentation process extends the shelf life of dairy products and makes them more digestible. Lot of individuals who are lactose intolerant can enjoy fermented dairy products because the lactose has been partially broken down into simpler sugars and lactic acid. Moreover, fermented dairy products are rich in probiotics, live microorganisms that provide health advantages to the host when taken in adequate amounts. These probiotics have been linked to improved gut health, enhanced immune function, and a reduced risk of certain chronic diseases. Additionally, fermentation can increase the levels of certain vitamins, including B vitamins and vitamin K2, and improve the bioavailability of minerals like calcium and magnesium.

The diversity of fermented dairy products is a testament to the versatility of the fermentation process. Yogurt, one of the most common fermented dairy products worldwide, is made by fermenting milk with a culture of Lactobacillus bulgaricus and also Streptococcus thermophilus. These bacteria produce lactic acid, which acts on milk proteins to give yogurt its characteristic tang and texture. Kefir, another widely consumed fermented dairy drink, is produced using kefir grains, a complex symbiotic matrix of bacteria and yeasts. The fermentation of kefir is more diverse, resulting in a product that contains not only lactic acid but also alcohol and carbon dioxide, contributing to its unique flavor and slightly effervescent quality.

Cheese production represents perhaps the most complex application of dairy fermentation. The process begins with the acidification of milk, either through the direct addition of lactic acid bacteria or through the action of bacteria naturally present in raw milk. Rennet, an enzyme complex, is then added to dissolve the milk, separating it into curds and whey. The curds, which contain the majority of the milk's fat and protein, are then pressed, aged, and sometimes further fermented with additional bacteria or molds, leading to the vast array of cheeses available today, each with its distinctive flavor, texture, and aroma.

Buttermilk and sour cream are examples of fermented dairy products that are traditionally made by allowing raw milk to naturally sour and thicken under controlled conditions. In commercial production, specific cultures of lactic acid bacteria are added to pasteurized milk to ensure safety and consistency. These products are prized for their creaminess and tang, adding depth to recipes and enjoyed on their own.

Producing fermented dairy products at home is both an art and a science, requiring careful attention to hygiene, temperature, and timing. The process typically begins with selecting high-quality, preferably pasteurized milk to ensure the absence of harmful bacteria. Cultures of the desired microorganisms are then introduced, and the milk is kept at a temperature conducive to fermentation, usually between 110°F and 115°F for yogurt. After fermentation, the product may be cooled and stored in the refrigerator to halt the process and preserve the freshness of the final product.

In conclusion, fermenting dairy products is a practice that beautifully blends tradition with biology, resulting in foods that are not only delicious and versatile but also beneficial for health. The process, driven by the activity of lactic acid bacteria, transforms the simple constituents of milk into a myriad of products that have sustained and delighted humans for millennia. Whether it's the creamy tang of yogurt, the enthusiasm of kefir, the rich complexity of cheese, or the smoothness of buttermilk, fermented dairy products continue to play a vital role in diets worldwide. As we explore and appreciate the wonders of fermentation, the enduring value of these ancient foods remains a testimony to the ingenuity of our ancestors and the enduring power of microbes to transform and enrich our food.

Fermenting Beverages

Fermenting beverages is a practice as old as civilization itself, with roots tracing back to the earliest human societies. This ancient craft harnesses the natural process of fermentation to transform various ingredients into drinks that are refreshing and flavorful and often enriched with health benefits. From the frothy bitters of beer to the complex notes of wine and the effervescent tang of kombucha, fermented beverages comprise a vast and varied category that spans cultures and continents. This section explores the art and science of fermenting beverages, including the basic principles of fermentation, the types of beverages that can be fermented, and the cultural significance of these drinks.

The process of fermenting beverages begins with fermentation, a metabolic phenomenon wherein microorganisms such as yeast and bacteria convert sugars into alcohol, carbon dioxide, and other metabolic byproducts. This biological process is the cornerstone of beverage fermentation, providing the means to preserve and transform a wide array of base ingredients, including grains, fruits, and even dairy, into consumable and often nutritious drinks. The specific microorganisms involved, the substrate they feed on, and the conditions under which fermentation occurs determine the type of beverage produced and its flavor profile.

Alcoholic beverages including beer, wine, and cider are among the most widely recognized fermentation products. Beer, one of the oldest and most universally consumed alcoholic drinks, is made by fermenting malted barley or other grains with water, hops, and yeast. The yeast metabolizes the sugars extracted from the grains, producing alcohol and carbon dioxide, while hops add bitterness and aroma, balancing the sweetness of the malt. Wine, another ancient beverage, is produced by fermenting the juice of crushed grapes. Yeasts, either naturally occurring on the grape skins or added during the winemaking process, convert the fructose found in the grape juice into alcohol and carbon dioxide. Cider involves a similar process, with apples or pears serving as the fermentable fruit base.

Non-alcoholic fermented beverages, such as kombucha, kefir, and certain types of fermented teas, have gained popularity for their probiotic properties and health benefits. Kombucha, a fermented tea drink, is produced by integrating a symbiotic culture of bacteria and yeast, also called SCOBY into sweetened tea. The culture ferments the tea, producing a slightly acidic, carbonated beverage rich in probiotics. Milk kefir and water kefir are fermented with kefir grains, which has lactic acid bacteria and yeasts in an array of proteins, lipids, as well as sugars. These beverages are praised for their beneficial effects on digestive health and immune system support.

The cultural significance of fermented beverages extends far beyond their nutritional value and refreshment. In many societies, these drinks hold ceremonial and social importance, embodying traditions and embodying the heritage of the communities that create them. For instance, wine has deep roots in religious ceremonies and celebrations worldwide, while beer is often associated with communal gatherings and social bonding. In many cultures, the production of fermented beverages is considered an art form, passed down through generations, with each region developing its unique variants and brewing techniques.

Creating fermented beverages requires knowledge, skill, and patience. The process typically begins with preparing the base ingredient, such as mashing grains for beer or pressing fruit for wine or cider. This is followed by adding yeast or another fermentation agent, which initiates the fermentation process. Temperature control is crucial, as too high or too low temperatures can inhibit fermentation or encourage the growth of undesirable microorganisms. The duration of fermentation differ depending on the beverage being produced and the desired outcome, ranging from a few days to several weeks or even months.

Quality control and sanitation are paramount in the production of fermented beverages. Contamination by unwanted bacteria or molds can spoil a batch, making it unsafe for consumption. As such, meticulous cleanliness and sterilized equipment are essential practices for commercial producers and home fermenters. Additionally, the art of tasting and blending allows brewers and winemakers to refine their products, achieving the desired balance of flavors and aromas.

In conclusion, fermenting beverages is a tradition that marries the biological magic of fermentation with human ingenuity and cultural expression. This process transforms simple ingredients into complex drinks that delight the senses, offer health benefits, and connect us to our cultural roots. Whether it's the crafting of a robust beer, the delicate fermentation of grapes into wine, or the brewing of probiotic-rich kombucha, the fermentation of beverages continues to be a vital and cherished practice across the globe. As we explore and experiment with new ingredients and methods, the world of fermented beverages expands, offering endless possibilities for innovation and enjoyment.

CHAPTER VI

Advanced Pickling and Fermentation

Experimenting with Flavor Combinations

Experimenting with flavor combinations through pickling and fermentation is an art form that dates back centuries, offering culinary enthusiasts the opportunity to explore a vast spectrum of tastes and textures. This ancient preservation technique not only extends the shelf life of food but also transforms the ingredients into something new and exciting, imbued with complex flavors that are not present in their raw state. The process of pickling and fermentation encourages creativity and innovation, as each batch can be tailored to suit individual palates or to complement specific dishes. This section delves into the nuances of experimenting with flavor combinations in pickling and fermentation, highlighting the endless possibilities these methods offer to the adventurous cook.

Pickling, at its core, involves submerging fruits, vegetables, or even meats in an acidic solution, typically vinegar-based, or a saltwater brine, to achieve preservation and flavor development. Fermentation, a closely related process, relies on the natural bacteria present in the food or added as a starter culture to break down sugars, producing lactic acid or alcohol. Both methods create an environment that inhibits the growth of spoilage-causing microorganisms, while the acids produced during the process impart a distinctive tangy taste.

One of the most exciting aspects of pickling and fermentation is the ability to experiment with a wide array of flavor combinations. This experimentation can begin with the choice of the base ingredient, which can range from common vegetables like cucumbers and cabbage to fruits, such as apples and cherries, and even include unconventional items like eggs or fish. The type of vinegar used in pickling can also significantly impact the flavor profile of the final product. For instance, apple cider vinegar introduces a fruity note, while rice vinegar offers a milder acidity suitable for delicate flavors.

Adding spices, herbs, and aromatics is where the real creativity comes into play. Traditional pickling spices include mustard seeds, coriander, dill, and black peppercorns, which can be used alone or in combination to create classic flavors. However, exploring beyond these staples can yield surprising and delightful results. For example, adding star anise and cinnamon to a pickling brine can infuse the produce with warm, aromatic notes, while a pinch of chili flakes or slices of fresh ginger adds heat and zing.

In fermentation, the flavors evolve and deepen over time, offering a different dimension to flavor experimentation. The type of salt used, the temperature at which fermentation occurs, and the duration of the process all influence the final taste. Incorporating fruits into vegetable ferments, such as adding apples to sauerkraut, can introduce a subtle sweetness that balances the acidity. Similarly, blending different vegetables, like combining beets with cabbage, creates a visually stunning product and layers the flavors.

The use of aromatic herbs and spices in fermentation can also transform the character of the fermented food. Fresh dill, basil, or mint can add a refreshing note to fermented vegetables, ideal for summer dishes. One might experiment with adding juniper berries, bay leaves, or cloves for a more robust flavor suitable for hearty winter meals. Including these aromatics enhances the taste and contributes to the fermented product's health benefits, as lot of herbs and spices are high in antioxidants and other beneficial compounds.

Exploring international cuisines provides further inspiration for flavor experimentation in pickling and fermentation. Korean kimchi, for example, with its combination of cabbage, radish, garlic, ginger, and gochugaru (Korean chili powder), offers an excellent model for creating spicy, deeply flavored ferments. Similarly, the Indian practice of pickling using a mix of spices like turmeric, fenugreek, and asafoetida can inspire bold and aromatic pickles that pair wonderfully with curries and rice dishes.

Experimenting with flavor combinations in pickling and fermentation is not without its challenges, but it also offers rewarding opportunities for discovery and innovation. It encourages cooks to think creatively about flavor profiles and consider how different spices, herbs, and aromatics interact with the base ingredients. Moreover, it invites an appreciation for the transformative power of microorganisms and the complex biochemical processes at play.

In conclusion, pickling and fermentation open up a world of flavor possibilities, allowing culinary enthusiasts to experiment with combinations that can elevate a simple meal to something extraordinary. Whether seeking to recreate traditional flavors or forge new culinary paths, pickling and fermentation provide a canvas for creativity. By embracing the unpredictability and variability inherent in these methods, cooks can discover unique and memorable flavors that reflect their personal tastes and culinary influences. As we continue to explore and experiment with these ancient techniques, we connect with our cultural heritage and contribute to the evolution of our global culinary landscape.

Creating Unique Fermentation Projects

Creating unique fermentation projects is an adventurous journey into the world of microbes, where culinary creativity meets the ancient art of preservation. Fermentation, a process used for thousands of years to preserve food and strengthen its nutritional value, has recently seen a resurgence among chefs, home cooks, and food enthusiasts seeking to explore new flavors and textures. This section delves into the art of crafting unique fermentation projects, highlighting the endless possibilities for innovation and the key considerations for success.

The essence of fermentation lies in the metabolic activity of microorganisms including bacteria, yeast, and molds, which convert sugars and starches into alcohol, acids, and other compounds. This natural process extends the shelf life of foods and imbues them with distinctive flavors, aromas, and health benefits. Embarking on unique fermentation projects involves harnessing these microbial processes to create novel and exciting food and drink experiences.

To begin a unique fermentation project, one must first understand the basic principles of fermentation, including the roles of various microorganisms, the importance of an anaerobic environment, and the factors influencing fermentation, such as temperature, pH, and salinity. With this foundational knowledge, enthusiasts can experiment with a wide range of ingredients beyond the traditional realms of sauerkraut, kimchi, and sourdough.

One innovative approach to unique fermentation projects is the exploration of unusual ingredient combinations. For instance, fermenting fruits with vegetables can yield unexpected and delightful results, such as pineapple and jalapeño kraut or apple and beet kvass. These combinations challenge traditional flavor profiles and offer opportunities to explore the nutritional synergies between different food groups.

Another avenue for creativity is incorporating global fermentation techniques into local ingredients. Drawing inspiration from traditional practices worldwide, such as the Japanese method of making miso or the Scandinavian technique of fermenting fish, can lead to creating culturally hybrid ferments that reflect a fusion of culinary traditions. For example, using a local variety of beans to make a miso-style paste or fermenting locally caught fish in the style of Swedish surströmming.

Experimenting with wild fermentation is yet another way to create unique fermentation projects. Wild fermentation relies on the naturally occurring microorganisms present on the ingredients and in the environment, rather than using commercially available starter cultures. This method can produce one-of-a-kind ferments that are a reflection of the local microbiome, adding a terroir-driven uniqueness to the project. For instance, capturing wild yeasts to create a unique sourdough starter or using the natural bacteria on cabbage leaves to ferment a batch of sauerkraut can yield products with flavors and textures that are truly unique to a specific location.

A key consideration in developing unique fermentation projects is the importance of experimentation and documentation. The variable nature of fermentation means that not all experiments will succeed as expected, but each attempt provides valuable learning opportunities. Keeping detailed records of recipes, ingredients, environmental conditions, and observations throughout the fermentation process can help refine techniques and replicate successful batches.

Safety is also paramount in fermentation projects. Understanding the signs of successful fermentation versus spoilage is crucial to ensure that the fermented foods are safe to consume. This includes recognizing the smell and appearance of healthy ferments, as well as being aware of the potential for contamination and how to avoid it, such as by maintaining clean workspaces, using sterilized equipment, and ensuring that fermentation vessels are properly sealed.

The potential for unique fermentation projects also extends into the realm of beverages. Creating novel fermented drinks, whether non-alcoholic like kombucha and kefir or alcoholic like mead and cider, allows for exploring different sugar sources, flavorings, and fermentation techniques. For example, fermenting herbal teas to create a flavored kombucha or using foraged fruits to brew a wild-fermented cider can result in beverages that are both innovative and reflective of the local environment.

In conclusion, creating unique fermentation projects is rewarding and blends science, art, and culinary creativity. By exploring unconventional ingredient combinations, incorporating global techniques, and embracing wild fermentation, enthusiasts can unlock a world of flavors and textures that challenge and expand the traditional boundaries of fermented foods and beverages. With a spirit of experimentation, a commitment to safety, and a willingness to learn from successes and failures, the possibilities for unique fermentation projects are as boundless as the microbial world. As we continue to delve into this fascinating realm, we enrich our culinary repertoire and deepen our connection to the natural processes that sustain and nourish us.

Incorporating Fermented Foods into Everyday Meals

Incorporating fermented foods into everyday meals is not just a culinary trend but a return to traditional eating practices that have sustained cultures around the globe for centuries. Fermentation, a process that naturally preserves food and enhances nutrient availability, offers many health benefits, including improved digestion and a stronger immune system. Beyond these advantages, fermented foods bring depth, complexity, and variety to the table, enriching our diets with tangy, savory, and utterly unique flavors. This section explores the art of integrating fermented foods into daily eating habits, offering insights into the benefits and versatility of these nutritional powerhouses.

Understanding their health benefits is the heart of incorporating fermented foods into meals. Fermented foods are high in probiotics, which are helpful bacteria that are crucial in maintaining gut health. A healthy gut microbiome is connected to numerous health outcomes, including enhanced digestion, reduced inflammation, and improved mental health. Fermentation also increases the bioavailability of nutrients, making it easier for the body to absorb vitamins as well as minerals from food. Additionally, the fermentation process can break down compounds that are difficult to digest, such as the lactose in milk, making fermented dairy products like yogurt and kefir more digestible for those with lactose intolerance.

The diversity of fermented foods available offers a palette from which to draw culinary inspiration. From the tangy crunch of sauerkraut and the spicy kick of kimchi to the creamy tang of yogurt and the effervescent fizz of kombucha, there is a fermented food to complement virtually any meal. Incorporating these foods into everyday eating requires both creativity and an openness to new flavors and textures.

One simple way to start is by adding fermented vegetables to salads and sandwiches. Sauerkraut, for example, can add a tangy crunch to a salad, while a few slices of pickled cucumber can transform a sandwich. Fermented vegetables can also serve as a flavorful side dish, offering a probiotic-rich alternative to traditional cooked vegetables. With its spicy and complex flavors,

Kimchi can be an excellent accompaniment to grilled meats or tofu, infusing the meal with the bold tastes of Korean cuisine.

Yogurt and kefir, with their creamy textures and mild acidity, are incredibly versatile and can be used in various dishes. A dollop of yogurt can cool the heat of spicy dishes, balance the sweetness of desserts, or serve as a base for smoothies and salad dressings. Kefir, slightly more tangy than yogurt, can be drunk on its own or used as a tenderizing marinade for meats. These fermented dairy products enhance the flavor of meals and contribute valuable nutrients, including calcium and protein.

Incorporating fermented grains and legumes can introduce new dimensions to staple dishes. With its distinctive tang and chewy texture, Sourdough bread can elevate a simple sandwich or serve as a hearty complement to soups and stews. Fermented legumes, such as tempeh, offer a nutritious and flavorful protein source for vegetarian and vegan dishes. Tempeh can be marinated, grilled, or added to stir-fries, bringing a savory depth to plant-based meals.

Beverages like kombucha and water kefir provide a probiotic-rich alternative to sugary drinks, offering refreshment with the added benefits of fermentation. These effervescent drinks can be enjoyed on their own or used as the base for creative mocktails, adding a lively twist to hydration.

The key to successfully incorporating fermented foods into meals is balance. The bold flavors of fermented foods can be overwhelming if used excessively, so it's important to pair them thoughtfully with other meal components. For example, the smoothness of yogurt can mellow the heat in spicy foods, while the acidity in pickled vegetables can cut through the rich flavor of fatty meats. Experimenting with small amounts and adjusting to taste can help find the perfect harmony between the fermented elements and the rest of the meal.

In conclusion, incorporating fermented foods into everyday meals is a delightful exploration of tradition, taste, and nutrition. These ancient foods, with their probiotic benefits and complex flavors, offer a simple yet profound way to enrich our diets and support our health. Whether it's by adding a spoonful of sauerkraut to a salad, enjoying a glass of kefir for breakfast, or savoring a slice of sourdough bread with dinner, the opportunities to integrate fermented foods into daily eating are limitless. As we rediscover the wisdom of traditional fermentation practices, we nourish our bodies and connect with the rich tapestry of culinary heritage that spans the globe. Embracing fermented foods in our meals is not just a dietary choice but a celebration of the diversity and creativity of human cuisine.

Aging and Storing Fermented Foods

Aging and storing fermented foods are crucial steps in the fermentation process that significantly impact the final product's flavor, texture, and shelf life. Fermentation, an ancient method of food preservation, involves the transformation of ingredients by microorganisms such as bacteria, yeast, and molds. This process extends the shelf life of perishable items and enriches them with unique flavors, textures, and health benefits. Proper aging and storage techniques are essential to ensure that these fermented products reach their full potential regarding taste and nutritional value. This section explores the intricacies of aging and storing fermented foods, highlighting the importance of these practices in the art of fermentation.

Aging, also referred to as maturation or ripening, is a critical phase in the production of many fermented foods, particularly cheeses, wines, and certain types of cured meats. During this phase, fermented products undergo a series of biochemical reactions that further develop their flavors, aromas, and textures. Aging conditions such as temperature, humidity, and exposure to oxygen are meticulously controlled to facilitate the activity of enzymes and microorganisms that contribute to the maturation process. For example, cheese aging can range from a few weeks to several years, with longer aging periods resulting in more complex flavor profiles and firmer textures. Similarly, wines matured in barrels or bottles develop depth and character over time, with the aging process allowing for the integration of flavors and softening of tannins.

The environment in which fermented foods are aged is paramount. Cheeses require specific humidity and temperature ranges to prevent drying out or the growth of unwanted molds. Wine cellars or temperature-controlled wine fridges offer the cool, stable conditions necessary for wine to age gracefully. A dark, cool pantry or cellar can provide an ideal aging environment for fermented vegetables and other products stored at room temperature. The goal is to create conditions that support the desired maturation processes while minimizing the risk of spoilage or deterioration.

Storage practices play an equally important role in preserving the quality and safety of fermented foods once they have reached their optimal level of maturity. Proper storage extends the shelf life of these products and maintains their nutritional and sensory qualities. Refrigeration is a common method for storing fermented foods, as the cold temperature slows down metabolic activity, helping preserve the product's texture and flavor. Foods such as yogurt, kefir, sauerkraut, and pickles can benefit from refrigeration, which keeps them safe and delicious for weeks or even months.

For long-term storage, some fermented products may require special conditions. For instance, hard cheeses can be waxed or vacuum-sealed and stored in a cool, humid environment to prevent drying out. Wines and certain types of beer benefit from being stored on their sides in a cool, dark place to keep the cork moist and prevent oxidation. Kombucha and other fermented beverages should be stored in airtight containers to maintain carbonation and prevent contamination.

When storing fermented foods, it is essential to monitor them for signs of spoilage, such as off-odors, discoloration, or the presence of mold. While many fermented products have a long shelf life due to their acidic environment, which inhibits the growth of harmful bacteria, they are not immune to spoilage. Proper sanitation practices, including the utilization of clean containers and utensils, can help prevent contamination and ensure the safety as well as quality of fermented foods.

Labeling is another important aspect of storing fermented foods, especially for home fermenters with multiple projects. Labels should include the production date, the product type, and any specific storage instructions. This practice helps keep track of aging times and ensures that foods are consumed within their optimal period of quality.

In conclusion, aging and storing fermented foods are artful practices that require knowledge, patience, and attention to detail. Through controlled aging, fermented foods develop complex flavors and textures that culinary enthusiasts highly prize. Proper storage ensures that these flavors are preserved and that the foods remain safe to consume. By adhering to best practices in aging and storage, artisans and home fermenters alike can maximize the potential of their fermented products, contributing to the rich tapestry of flavors that define this ancient culinary tradition. Whether savoring a piece of aged cheese, a glass of meticulously matured wine, or a crisp, tangy pickle, the rewards of well-aged and properly stored fermented foods are a testament to the time-honored processes that bring them to our tables.

CHAPTER VII

Health Benefits and Nutritional Value

Probiotics and Gut Health

The art of pickling and fermentation, practices as ancient as human civilization itself, have transcended their initial purpose of food preservation to become recognized for significant health benefits, particularly in the realm of probiotics and gut health. These traditional methods extend the shelf life of foods and enhance their nutritional value, introducing beneficial bacteria that take part to a healthy digestive system. This section delves into the health benefits and nutritional value of pickled and fermented foods, focusing on their role in promoting gut health and the mechanisms by which they exert their positive effects.

At the core of the health benefits associated with fermented foods is their rich content of probiotics, live microorganisms that offer health advantages on the host when consumed in adequate amounts. Probiotics, primarily found in fermented dairy products like yogurt and kefir, as well as in non-dairy fermented foods including sauerkraut, kimchi, and miso, are crucial in maintaining a balanced gut microbiota. This balanced microbial ecosystem is essential for various bodily functions, including digestion, nutrient absorption, and immune system modulation.

The process of fermentation transforms the substrate (the base ingredient being fermented) in several ways that benefit human health. First, the lactic acid bacteria involved in fermentation generate enzymes that break down nutrients into a more digestible forms. For instance, the lactose found in milk is broken down into simpler sugars like glucose as well as galactose, making fermented dairy products more digestible for individuals with lactose intolerance. Additionally, fermentation can increase the availability of vitamins and minerals for absorption, particularly B vitamins, including B12, which is often difficult to obtain from plant-based sources.

Fermented foods also act as natural probiotic supplements. The consumption of these foods introduces beneficial bacteria directly into the gut, where they can help restore the balance of gut flora. A healthy gut microbiota is associated with numerous health advantages, like improved digestion, enhanced immune function, as well as a reduced risk of particular chronic diseases. Probiotics have been shown to alleviate conditions including inflammatory bowel disease, diarrhea, as well as irritable bowel syndrome. They may also play a role in preventing allergies and maintaining a healthy weight.

Moreover, fermentation produces metabolites such as short-chain fatty acids (SCFAs), including butyrate, acetate, and propionate. These compounds have been shown to have anti-inflammatory properties, strengthen the gut barrier function, and modulate the immune response. SCFAs serve as energy sources for colonocytes (the cells lining the colon), promoting their health and integrity, which is crucial for preventing pathogens from entering the bloodstream.

Beyond gut health, the benefits of fermented foods extend to mental health, with emerging research suggesting a connection between the gut microbiota and the brain, often called as the "gut-brain axis." Probiotics from fermented foods may influence brain health by producing neurotransmitters, reducing inflammation, and modulation of the stress response. This fascinating area of study opens up potential avenues for using fermented foods as part of dietary strategies to support mental well-being.

While the benefits of fermented foods are clear, it is essential to note that not all pickled foods offer the same probiotic and nutritional advantages. Quick pickling methods that use vinegar rather than natural fermentation do not foster the growth of probiotics. However, these foods still provide nutritional benefits, such as preserving vitamins and adding antioxidants from the vinegar and spices used in the pickling process. To reap the full health benefits, including probiotics, consuming naturally fermented foods that have undergone a transformation facilitated by beneficial bacteria is essential.

Combining fermented foods into the diet can be simple and delicious. From adding sauerkraut to sandwiches and salads to enjoying a serving of yogurt or kefir for breakfast, there are numerous ways to enjoy the flavors and health benefits of these foods. As with any dietary change, it's advisable to introduce fermented foods gradually to allow the digestive system to adjust to the increased intake of probiotics.

In conclusion, the health benefits as well as nutritional value of pickling and fermentation are vast, with a significant impact on gut health being among the most celebrated advantages. The probiotics provided by naturally fermented foods contribute to a balanced gut microbiota, which in turn supports digestion, immune function, and even mental health. By embracing the ancient practices of pickling and fermentation, we connect with culinary traditions passed down through generations and access the profound health benefits these methods offer. As research uncovers the intricate connections between diet, gut health, and overall health, the role of fermented foods in promoting health and preventing disease becomes increasingly clear, highlighting the timeless wisdom embedded in these traditional practices.

Increased Nutrient Availability

The process of pickling and fermentation, a cornerstone of culinary traditions across cultures, serves as a method for preserving food and significantly enhances its nutritional profile. Increased nutrient availability is a compelling advantage among the myriad health benefits attributed to these ancient practices. This section explores how pickling and fermentation improve the nutritional value of foods by making vitamins and minerals more accessible to the human body, thereby contributing to overall health and well-being.

At the heart of the fermentation process is the action of beneficial microorganisms such as bacteria, yeast, and molds. These microorganisms break down complex compounds in food into more digestible forms, a transformation that inherently increases the bioavailability of nutrients. Lactic acid fermentation, in particular, is celebrated for enhancing the nutritional content of foods. This type of fermentation is facilitated by lactic acid bacteria, which alter sugars into lactic acid, an environment that not only preserves the food but also promotes the production of enzymes and the breakdown of anti-nutritional factors.

One of the primary benefits of fermentation is the increased availability of B vitamins. Fermented foods including kefir, yogurt, tempeh, and sauerkraut are rich sources of B vitamins, including B12, riboflavin (B2), thiamine (B1), and niacin (B3). These vitamins are crucial in energy metabolism, nerve function, as well as the synthesis of red blood cells. For vegetarians as well as vegans, who may have limited sources of vitamin B12, fermented foods can be an invaluable addition to the diet, providing essential nutrients that are otherwise found in animal products.

Fermentation also enhances the mineral content of foods, particularly calcium, magnesium, and iron, by reducing the levels of phytic acid, a natural compound found in plant seeds which binds to minerals and inhibits their absorption. Through the action of lactic acid bacteria, phytic acid is broken down, freeing up minerals and making them more accessible to the body. This process is particularly beneficial in plant-based diets, where mineral absorption can be a concern.

Moreover, producing short-chain fatty acids (SCFAs) during fermentation has significant health implications. SCFAs, such as butyrate, propionate, and acetate, are produced when gut bacteria ferment certain dietary fibers. These fatty acids serve as energy sources for colon cells, help maintain the integrity of the gut barrier, and possess anti-inflammatory properties. SCFAs in the gut are linked to reduced risk of inflammatory diseases, obesity, and type 2 diabetes, highlighting the integral role of fermented foods in gut health and systemic inflammation.

While often associated with vinegar-based preservation, pickling can also involve fermentation, leading to similar nutritional enhancements. Fermented pickles, as opposed to those simply soaked in vinegar, undergo a process that generates beneficial bacteria and increases nutrient availability. These pickles not only add a probiotic boost to the diet but also provide vitamins and minerals in more absorbable forms.

Despite these benefits, it's essential to recognize that not all fermented and pickled foods are created equal. Commercially produced items may contain high sodium or added sugars levels, which can detract from their health benefits. Additionally, some pickling processes use pasteurization to ensure shelf stability, which can destroy probiotics and enzymes beneficial for health. Therefore, choosing traditionally fermented and minimally processed foods is key to maximizing the health advantages of pickling and fermentation.

Incorporating fermented and pickled foods into the diet can be both simple and delicious. From adding a serving of sauerkraut to a sandwich to including a dollop of yogurt in a smoothie, these foods offer versatile and flavorful ways to enhance nutrient intake. As with any dietary change, it's advisable to introduce fermented foods gradually to allow the digestive system to adjust, especially for individuals who may not be accustomed to the high probiotic content of these foods.

In conclusion, the increased nutrient availability resulting from pickling and fermentation represents a significant health benefit of these time-honored practices. By breaking down antinutritional factors and enhancing the bioavailability of vitamins and minerals, fermentation makes it easier for the body to absorb important nutrients. Furthermore, the process contributes to gut health through the production of beneficial bacteria and SCFAs, underscoring the holistic impact of fermented and pickled foods on overall well-being. As we continue to explore and embrace these traditional methods of food preservation, we not only connect with our culinary heritage but also access the profound nutritional benefits they offer, enriching our diets and supporting our health in a myriad of ways.

Other Health Benefits of Pickled and Fermented Foods

Pickled and fermented foods have been staples in global cuisines for centuries, celebrated not only for their unique flavors and ability to preserve the bounty of the harvest but also for their numerous health benefits. Beyond the well-known advantages of improved gut health and increased nutrient availability, these foods offer many other health benefits contributing to overall well-being. This section delves into the lesser-discussed yet equally essential health benefits of pickled and fermented foods, shedding light on their role in disease prevention, mental health, and immune system support.

One of the significant health benefits of pickled and fermented foods is their potential role in disease prevention. The fermentation process generates a wide array of bioactive compounds, including antioxidants, which can neutralize harmful free radicals in the body. Free radicals are referred to as unstable molecules that can cause oxidative stress, resulting in cellular damage and the onset of chronic diseases including heart disease, cancer, and neurodegenerative disorders. The antioxidants present in fermented foods, such as vitamin C in sauerkraut or the polyphenols in red wine, can help mitigate this risk, offering protective effects against disease.

Moreover, certain fermented foods have been shown to have anti-carcinogenic properties. For example, studies have suggested that consuming fermented dairy products like yogurt and kefir may reduce the risk of bladder cancer, while the probiotics found in these foods can inhibit the growth of Helicobacter pylori, a bacterium linked with stomach cancer. Similarly, the glucosinolates found in fermented cruciferous vegetables like kimchi are broken down into compounds that have been studied for their cancer-preventive effects.

The impact of pickled and fermented foods on mental health is another area of growing interest within the scientific community. The gut-brain axis, a complex communication network linking the gastrointestinal tract and the brain, is critical in mental health. The beneficial bacteria in fermented foods can produce neurotransmitters, including serotonin and gamma-aminobutyric acid (or GABA), which influence mood and cognitive functions. Regular consumption of these foods may add to improved mental well-being, reducing symptoms of anxiety and depression. Additionally, the probiotics in fermented foods can modulate the body's stress response, potentially offering resilience against stress-related mental health issues.

Immune system support is another health benefit of pickled and fermented foods. A huge portion of the body's immune system is located in the gut, where a diverse community of microbes interacts with immune cells. The probiotics in fermented foods can enhance the body's defense mechanisms by strengthening the gut barrier, preventing the entry of pathogens, and modulating the immune response. For example, specific strains of lactic acid bacteria have been shown to stimulate the production of antibodies and activate immune cells, providing a natural boost to the immune system.

Furthermore, fermented foods can contribute to weight management and metabolic health. The probiotics and SCFAs produced during fermentation can influence metabolism, with research suggesting a link between gut microbiota composition and obesity. These microbial byproducts can affect energy extraction from food, fat storage, and appetite regulation, potentially aiding in weight loss and preventing metabolic diseases such as type 2 diabetes. Additionally, the high fiber content of many fermented vegetable products can promote satiety, reduce calorie intake, and support healthy digestion.

It's important to note that while pickled and fermented foods offer numerous health benefits, moderation is key. Some pickled foods can be high in sodium, which may contribute to hypertension if consumed in excess. Similarly, certain fermented alcoholic beverages should be enjoyed in moderation due to the health risks associated with excessive alcohol consumption. Choosing low-sodium options and consuming various fermented foods can help maximize the health benefits while reducing potential risks.

In conclusion, the health benefits of pickled and fermented foods extend far beyond gut health and nutrient availability. These traditional food preservation methods offer protective effects against chronic diseases, support mental well-being, bolster the immune system, and can play a role in weight management and metabolic health. By incorporating a diverse range of pickled and fermented foods into the diet, individuals can tap into the ancient wisdom of fermentation to enrich their diets and enhance their health in multiple dimensions. As research continues to unravel the complex interactions between diet, microbiota, and health, the value of these time-honored foods in promoting overall well-being becomes increasingly clear, underscoring the importance of maintaining the culinary traditions that have nourished human societies for generations.

Addressing Safety Concerns

Addressing safety concerns in pickled and fermented foods is a crucial aspect of ensuring that these ancient preservation techniques enhance flavor and nutritional value and maintain food safety standards. While fermentation and pickling have been practiced for centuries as reliable methods to preserve food, improper handling or preparation can lead to health risks. This section explores the safety concerns associated with pickled and fermented foods, highlighting the measures that can be taken to mitigate these risks and ensure the safe consumption of these nutritious and flavorful products.

The process of fermentation relies on the growth of beneficial microorganisms to transform food, making it less susceptible to spoilage and pathogenic bacteria. However, the success of this process depends on creating the correct conditions for these beneficial microbes to thrive while inhibiting harmful ones. One of the primary safety concerns in fermenting foods is the potential growth of pathogenic bacteria, such as Clostridium botulinum, which produces toxins that can cause botulism, a rare but possibly fatal illness. This risk is mainly associated with foods that are fermented in an anaerobic (oxygen-free) environment, which is conducive to the growth of C. botulinum.

To mitigate the risk of botulism and other bacterial infections, it is essential to follow proper fermentation practices. This includes using clean, sterilized equipment and containers to prevent contamination, ensuring the fermentation vessels are properly sealed to create an anaerobic environment, and maintaining the fermentation at the correct temperature. The acidity of the fermenting environment is also crucial; a pH of 4.6 or lower inhibits the growth of harmful bacteria. Ensuring safety during fermentation can be achieved by monitoring the pH levels and adjusting them with vinegar or citric acid.

Another safety concern in pickling and fermentation is the presence of mycotoxins, toxic substances produced by molds that can grow on improperly stored or fermented foods. While certain molds are used in the fermentation of foods like cheese and soy sauce and are safe to consume, others can be harmful. It is important to keep the fermenting food submerged in its brine or liquid to prevent mold growth, as exposure to air can encourage mold development. If mold appears on the surface of a fermenting food, it should be removed immediately, and the food should be discarded if the mold has penetrated below the surface.

The use of adequate salt concentrations in pickling is another key factor in ensuring food safety. Salt inhibits the growth of undesirable microorganisms by creating a hostile environment for them while promoting the growth of beneficial lactic acid bacteria. However, too much salt can also inhibit the fermentation process, so following recommended salt-to-water ratios in recipes is important.

Cross-contamination is a further safety concern that can occur during the preparation of pickled and fermented foods. Using utensils or containers that have come into contact with raw meat, poultry, or fish can introduce harmful bacteria to the pickled or fermented foods. To avoid cross-contamination, utensils and containers should be thoroughly washed and sanitized between uses, and separate cutting boards should be used for different types of food.

Despite these safety concerns, it is essential to recognize that cases of foodborne illness linked to properly prepared pickled and fermented foods are scarce. The lactic acid bacteria involved in fermentation produce acids that lower the pH of the food, creating a setting that is hostile to pathogenic bacteria. Additionally, the salt used in pickling further hinders microbial growth.

To ensure the safety of pickled and fermented foods, consumers and producers alike should adhere to best practices for food safety, including proper hygiene, temperature control, and pH monitoring. For those new to pickling and fermentation, starting with tried-and-true recipes from reputable sources and paying close attention to the signs of successful fermentation, such as the presence of bubbles and a tangy aroma, can help avoid common pitfalls.

In conclusion, while pickling and fermentation are time-honored techniques that offer numerous health benefits and culinary possibilities, attention to food safety is paramount. By understanding and addressing the potential safety concerns associated with these methods, enthusiasts can enjoy their labor's delicious and nutritious products with peace of mind. Proper preparation, cleanliness, and adherence to safety guidelines are key to harnessing the transformative power of fermentation while ensuring the well-being of those who partake in these preserved delights. As interest in traditional food preservation methods grows, so does the importance of educating both producers and consumers about the practices that will keep pickled and fermented foods safe and enjoyable for everyone.

CHAPTER VIII

Sustainability and Self-Sufficiency

Reducing Food Waste through Pickling and Fermentation

Reducing food waste has become a critical environmental and economic issue in the modern era. As societies search for sustainable solutions to this challenge, traditional methods such as pickling and fermentation have re-emerged as effective strategies. These ancient practices, which extend the shelf life of perishable food items by harnessing the power of natural preservation processes, offer a practical and eco-friendly approach to minimizing food waste. This section explores how pickling and fermentation can reduce food waste, the benefits of these methods, and their impact on sustainability.

Pickling and fermentation are processes that preserve food through the action of acidification or the activity of beneficial microorganisms. In pickling, food is submerged in an acidic solution, typically vinegar, or a saltwater brine, creating an environment that inhibits the development of spoilage-causing bacteria. Conversely, fermentation relies on the natural fermentation process where microorganisms including yeast and bacteria convert sugars into alcohol, lactic acid, or acetic acid. Both methods not only preserve the food but also enhance its nutritional value and introduce a variety of new flavors.

One of the key ways in which pickling and fermentation reduce food waste is by extending the shelf life of vegetables, fruits, dairy, and even meats. Many perishable items that might otherwise spoil before they can be consumed can be transformed into products that last for months or even years. This longevity allows for a more efficient use of food resources, reducing the need to discard items that are not immediately consumed. For example, surplus vegetables from a garden harvest can be pickled or fermented, supplying nutritious food long after the growing season has ended.

Furthermore, pickling and fermentation can utilize parts of food that are often discarded. Vegetable peels, stems, and leaves, which might typically be thrown away, can be transformed into delicious and nutritious pickled dishes. This minimizes waste and encourages a more holistic approach to food consumption, where every part of the plant is valued and utilized. For instance, watermelon rind, which is commonly discarded, can be pickled to create a crunchy, flavorful snack.

These preservation methods also contribute to food security by providing a reliable food source that is not dependent on refrigeration. This is particularly beneficial in areas with limited electricity access or during natural disasters when power outages may occur. Fermented and pickled foods can be safely stored at room temperature, ensuring people can access nutritious food even in challenging circumstances.

The environmental benefits of reducing food waste through pickling and fermentation are significant. Food waste contributes to a large portion of the waste in landfills, where it decomposes and releases methane, a potent greenhouse gas. By preserving food and extending its shelf life, the amount of waste sent to landfills is minimized, thereby decreasing methane emissions. Moreover, by making the most of food resources, pickling and fermentation support more sustainable food systems that minimize the environmental impact of agriculture and food production.

Culturally, pickling and fermentation also play a role in reducing food waste by promoting the value of preserved foods. Many cultures have long traditions of fermenting and pickling, not only as a means of preservation but also as a way to celebrate seasonal and local foods. By embracing these practices, communities can foster a greater appreciation for the diversity of flavors that preserved foods offer, encouraging a shift in perception where preserved foods are seen as desirable and valuable rather than as mere alternatives to fresh produce.

Adopting pickling and fermentation as strategies to reduce food waste requires some knowledge and skill, but it is accessible to everyone willing to learn. Numerous resources, from books to online tutorials, are available to guide beginners through the process. It is also a practice that encourages creativity and experimentation, as individuals can explore different flavor combinations and techniques to create personalized preserved foods.

In conclusion, pickling and fermentation represent powerful tools in the fight against food waste. Extending the shelf life of perishable items, transforming often-discarded food parts into edible treats, and offering an alternative to refrigeration-dependent preservation methods contribute to environmental sustainability and food security. Furthermore, they enrich our culinary traditions, inviting us to explore and savor the depth of flavors that preserved foods can offer. As society grapples with food waste challenges, the ancient art of pickling and fermentation stand out as relevant and valuable solutions, blending tradition with innovation to create a more sustainable and flavorful future.

Harnessing Seasonal Produce

Harnessing seasonal produce through pickling and fermentation is a practice that allows for the enjoyment of fresh flavors throughout the year and connects us to the cycles of nature and the bounty of each season. This traditional method of preservation, deeply rooted in cultures worldwide, offers a sustainable way to reduce food waste, enhance nutritional intake, and diversify culinary experiences. This section delves into the significance of utilizing seasonal produce for pickling and fermentation, exploring the benefits, challenges, and the profound connection it fosters between our diets and the natural world.

Seasonal produce offers the freshest and most flavorful ingredients for pickling and fermentation, as fruits and vegetables are at their peak of ripeness. This ensures a superior taste profile in the preserved product and maximizes the nutritional content. Vitamins, minerals, and antioxidants are most abundant in produce harvested in season, and by preserving these foods at their prime, we can retain these essential nutrients. Fermentation can further enhance the bioavailability of these nutrients, making them more accessible to the body.

The act of preserving seasonal produce through pickling and fermentation is a testament to human ingenuity in lengthening the shelf life of perishable foods. Before the advent of modern refrigeration, these methods were indispensable for ensuring a stable food supply throughout the year, especially in regions with harsh winters or dry seasons. Today, they serve not only as a means of food preservation but also as a way to reduce waste by capturing the surplus of seasonal harvests that might otherwise spoil.

However, harnessing seasonal produce for preservation is not without its challenges. It requires planning and knowledge of both the fermentation and pickling processes and an understanding of the seasonality of different fruits and vegetables. Timing is crucial, as capturing produce at its peak requires attentiveness to local growing seasons and may involve a concentrated effort to prepare and preserve large quantities of food within a short time frame. Despite these challenges, the rewards of preserving seasonal produce are manifold, offering a tangible connection to the rhythm of nature and the local environment.

One of the most significant benefits of using seasonal produce for pickling and fermentation is the ability to enjoy the flavors of specific seasons year-round. Cucumbers pickled in brine, tomatoes fermented into salsa, or peaches preserved in vinegar can bring the taste of summer to the winter table. Similarly, autumn's apples can be transformed into cider or sauerkraut, providing a taste of fall during the spring and summer months. This adds variety to the diet and allows for culinary creativity, as cooks can experiment with different flavor combinations and preservation techniques.

Moreover, pickling and fermenting seasonal produce supports local agriculture and sustainability. Individuals can reduce the carbon footprint associated with transporting food over long distances by sourcing ingredients from local farmers' markets or community-supported agriculture (or CSA) programs. This practice promotes a more sustainable food system that values local ecosystems and the labor of those who cultivate the land. It also fosters a sense of community, as individuals come together to share recipes, techniques, and the fruits of their labor.

The cultural significance of pickling and fermenting seasonal produce cannot be overstated. Many cultures have unique traditions and recipes for preserving foods, passed down through generations. Engaging in these practices allows individuals to connect with their heritage and explore the culinary traditions of other cultures. Whether it's making kimchi in the Korean tradition, fermenting cucumbers into Russian-style pickles, or preparing Italian giardiniera, each preserved dish tells a story of cultural identity and culinary history.

Incorporating pickled and fermented seasonal produce into the diet also offers health benefits. The probiotics generated during fermentation can improve gut health, while the acids and enzymes present in pickled foods can aid digestion. Additionally, the preservation process can increase the availability of certain nutrients, making these foods delicious and nutritious additions to meals.

In conclusion, harnessing seasonal produce through pickling and fermentation is a practice rich in benefits and steeped in tradition. It allows us to capture the essence of each season, reduce food waste, support local agriculture, and explore the depths of culinary creativity. By embracing these age-old preservation methods, we deepen our connection to the natural world, celebrate cultural heritage, and nourish our bodies with seasonal produce's vibrant flavors and nutrients. As we continue to explore and innovate within the realms of pickling and fermentation, we reaffirm our commitment to sustainability, community, and the timeless art of preserving the earth's bounty.

Preserving Harvest Surplus

Preserving harvest surplus through pickling and fermentation is an ancient tradition that has seen a resurgence in modern times, offering a sustainable and flavorful way to extend the life of seasonal bounty. This practice ensures that the abundance of fruits and vegetables harvested at their peak can be enjoyed year-round. It also reduces food waste and supports a more sustainable food system. In this section, we explore the multifaceted benefits of using pickling and fermentation to preserve harvest surplus, the processes involved, and the cultural significance of these preservation methods.

At the heart of pickling and fermentation is the basic principle of using salt, sugar, acid, and sometimes cultures of beneficial bacteria to inhibit spoilage and transform the texture, flavor, and nutritional profile of foods. Pickling often involves submerging the produce in an acidic solution, such as vinegar, along with various spices and seasonings to achieve a desired flavor. Conversely, fermentation relies on the natural or added microorganisms to convert sugars and starches in the food into alcohol or acids, naturally preserving the food and enriching it with probiotics, vitamins, and enzymes.

One of the primary benefits of preserving harvest surplus through these methods is reducing food waste. In many parts of the world, a significant portion of harvested produce never reaches the consumer due to spoilage, overproduction, or market demand fluctuations. By pickling or fermenting excess fruits and vegetables, individuals and communities can significantly reduce the amount of food discarded, turning potential waste into nutritious and delicious food items. This conserves resources and contributes to food security by providing a stable supply of preserved foods that can be consumed during off-seasons or in times of scarcity.

Moreover, pickling and fermentation can enhance the nutritional value of the preserved produce. Fermented foods, in particular, are renowned for their health benefits, like improved digestion and gut health, due to the presence of live probiotics. These beneficial bacteria can aid in the breakdown of food components, making nutrients more accessible and absorption more efficient. Furthermore, the fermentation process can increase the levels of particular vitamins, such as B vitamins, and introduce unique metabolites with potential health-promoting properties.

The versatility of pickling and fermentation allows for a wide range of produce to be preserved, from cucumbers, carrots, and cabbages to fruits like apples, pears, and berries. This diversity enables individuals to experiment with flavors and techniques, creating custom blends that reflect personal tastes and culinary traditions. For example, one might pickle green beans with dill and garlic for a classic flavor, or ferment hot peppers with onions and carrots for a spicy salsa that can be used as a condiment or ingredient in various dishes.

The cultural significance of preserving harvest surplus through pickling and fermentation cannot be overstated. These practices are deeply embedded in many cultural traditions, serving as a link to heritage and ancestral knowledge. From the kimchi of Korea to the sauerkraut of Germany, pickled and fermented foods play a central role in national cuisines, celebrations, and daily meals. Engaging in these preservation methods allows individuals to connect with their cultural roots, explore the culinary traditions of others, and participate in a global community of preservation enthusiasts.

Implementing pickling and fermentation as strategies for preserving harvest surplus requires some basic knowledge and skills, but it is accessible to beginners and can be adapted to suit individual needs and resources. Key considerations include choosing fresh, high-quality produce; using clean, sterilized equipment; and following reliable recipes to ensure safety and success. It is also important to store preserved foods properly in cool, dark places to maintain their quality and extend their shelf life.

In conclusion, preserving harvest surplus through pickling and fermentation offers a practical and enjoyable way to reduce food waste, enhance nutrition, and celebrate cultural traditions. These age-old methods of food preservation empower individuals to take an active role in managing their food resources, promoting sustainability, and exploring the rich tapestry of flavors that pickled and fermented foods bring to the table. As we continue to face global challenges connected to food security and waste, the revival of pickling and fermentation stands as a testament to the enduring wisdom of traditional food practices and their relevance in today's world.

Economic and Environmental Benefits

The resurgence of interest in traditional food preservation methods, particularly pickling and fermentation, reflects a growing recognition of their economic and environmental benefits. These ancient practices extend the shelf life of perishable food items through natural processes and offer sustainable solutions to contemporary challenges related to food waste, resource conservation, and health. This section explores the multifaceted economic and environmental advantages of pickling and fermentation, underscoring their significance in promoting a more sustainable and health-conscious food system.

Economically, pickling and fermentation provide cost-effective means of preserving food. These methods can lead to considerable savings for households and communities by reducing the need to purchase fresh produce out of season, when prices are typically higher due to transportation and storage costs. By pickling or fermenting seasonal produce when it is abundant and inexpensive, consumers can enjoy a diverse diet throughout the year without incurring the premium associated with off-season produce. Furthermore, these preservation techniques allow individuals to capitalize on bulk purchasing or harvesting, transforming surplus fruits and vegetables into valuable food products that can be stored and consumed over time.

The economic benefits of pickling and fermentation extend beyond household savings to include potential income generation. Artisanal pickles, fermented beverages, and specialty condiments have gained popularity in local and global markets, offering small- scale producers and entrepreneurs opportunities to develop unique food products. The low start-up and operational costs associated with these preservation methods make them accessible to many individuals, including those in resource-limited settings. Producers can create sustainable livelihoods by tapping into the growing demand for natural, probiotic-rich, and artisanal foods while contributing to the diversity and resilience of local food economies.

Environmentally, pickling and fermentation are crucial in reducing food waste, a pressing issue with significant implications for resource use and greenhouse gas emissions. According to estimates from UN Food and Agriculture Organization, almost one-third of the food generated worldwide is lost or wasted. Pickling and fermentation can greatly reduce the amount of food which ends up in landfills, where it breaks down and emits methane, a powerful greenhouse gas, by prolonging the shelf life of perishable goods. Therefore, these preservation methods contribute to mitigating climate change by minimizing methane emissions associated with food waste.

Moreover, pickling and fermentation contribute to environmental sustainability by reducing reliance on energy-intensive storage and transportation infrastructure. Refrigeration and cold chain logistics, while essential for preserving fresh produce, consume considerable amounts of energy and contribute to carbon emissions. In contrast, pickled and fermented foods can be stored at ambient temperatures for extended periods, reducing the need for refrigeration and the associated energy use. This attribute makes pickling and fermentation particularly valuable in regions with limited electricity access or where reducing energy consumption is a priority.

The environmental benefits of pickling and fermentation are further amplified when these practices are combined with sustainable farming and sourcing practices. Utilizing locally sourced, organic produce for pickling and fermentation can minimize the environmental impacts associated with conventional agriculture, such as pesticide use and soil degradation. Additionally, these preservation methods can help valorize underutilized or imperfect produce that might not meet the aesthetic standards of commercial markets, further reducing food waste and supporting biodiversity by encouraging the cultivation of a wider variety of crops.

Culturally, the revival of pickling and fermentation fosters a more profound connection to food and its origins, encouraging a more mindful and sustainable approach to consumption. By engaging in these practices, individuals and communities become active participants in the food system, gaining an appreciation for the seasonality of produce, the labor involved in food production, and the value of preserving food traditions. This cultural shift towards valuing and preserving food can have broad implications for environmental sustainability, as it promotes behaviors that prioritize resource conservation, waste reduction, and ecological balance.

In conclusion, the economic and environmental benefits of pickling and fermentation highlight the relevance of these ancient food preservation methods in addressing contemporary challenges. By offering cost-effective, low-energy solutions to food waste and providing opportunities for sustainable livelihoods, pickling and fermentation contribute to a more resilient and environmentally responsible food system. As society grapples with the dual imperatives of economic sustainability and environmental stewardship, the practices of pickling and fermentation stand as a testament to the wisdom of traditional knowledge and the potential for innovative approaches to shaping a more sustainable future.

CHAPTER IX

Integrating Pickling and Fermentation into Lifestyle

Incorporating Homemade Pickles and Ferments into Meals

Incorporating homemade pickles and ferments into meals is not just a culinary trend but a lifestyle choice that celebrates tradition, nutrition, and sustainability. The art of pickling and fermentation transforms ordinary ingredients into extraordinary complements that enhance everyday dishes' flavor and nutritional value. This section explores how homemade pickles and ferments can be integrated into meals, highlighting the health benefits, culinary diversity, and the joy of creating and sharing these traditional foods.

The process of pickling and fermentation dates back thousands of years, serving as a fundamental food preservation technique across various cultures. Today, these methods are revered for their preservative qualities and their health benefits, including improved gut health, enhanced nutrient absorption, and the introduction of probiotics into the diet. Homemade pickles and ferments are free from artificial preservatives and excessive sodium, common in commercial versions, making them a healthier option for those looking to enrich their diet with fermented foods.

Incorporating homemade pickles and ferments into meals is remarkably versatile, offering a range of flavors from tangy and crisp to rich and umami-packed. Depending on the meal and the type of pickle or ferment, they can serve as a condiment, side dish, flavor enhancer, or even a main ingredient. For instance, a simple sandwich or burger can be elevated with the addition of crunchy, homemade pickled cucumbers or onions, adding a burst of flavor and texture. Similarly, a dollop of fermented sauerkraut or kimchi can transform a plate of grilled sausages or a bowl of rice into a probiotic-rich, flavorful meal.

Salads and bowls offer another canvas for the inclusion of pickles and ferments. A salad dressed with pickled beets or carrots can introduce a delightful sweet and sour element, balancing the freshness of the greens. Grain bowls or Buddha bowls benefit significantly from the addition of fermented vegetables, lending depth and complexity to these wholesome dishes. The acidity of pickles and the savory notes of ferments like miso can also act as a natural flavor enhancer, reducing the need for additional salt or dressings.

Homemade pickles and ferments can also be creatively used in dips, spreads, and sauces. For example, blending fermented vegetables into hummus can add an unexpected twist to the classic dip, introducing new flavors and increasing its probiotic content. Similarly, a sauce or dressing made with homemade pickle brine can infuse dishes with a unique tangy flavor, perfect for drizzling over roasted vegetables, salads, or grilled meats.

Breakfast, often overlooked in discussions about pickles and ferments, presents an opportunity to start the day with a probiotic boost. A serving of yogurt or kefir, fermented dairy products, can be the foundation of a nutritious breakfast bowl, topped with fruits, nuts, and a drizzle of honey. Fermented condiments, such as salsa or chutney, can add zest to scrambled eggs or avocado toast, making the day's first meal both delicious and beneficial for gut health.

Integrating homemade pickles and ferments into meals reflects a commitment to sustainability and reducing food waste. By preserving seasonal produce at its peak, these methods allow for the enjoyment of flavors that would otherwise be fleeting, extending the life of fruits and vegetables that might have gone to waste. Furthermore, the process of creating pickles and ferments from scratch fosters a connection to the food we eat, encouraging mindfulness and appreciation for the ingredients and the work involved in their transformation.

In conclusion, incorporating homemade pickles and ferments into meals is an enriching practice that spans cultures and cuisines, offering endless possibilities for culinary exploration. Beyond their health benefits and role in food preservation, pickles and ferments add vibrancy and complexity to dishes, inviting creativity and experimentation in the kitchen. Whether used as a condiment, side, or integral part of a dish, these traditional foods can transform the ordinary into the extraordinary, making every meal an opportunity to celebrate the art and science of fermentation. As we continue to rediscover and embrace these age-old techniques, we enrich our diets and contribute to a more sustainable as well as health-conscious approach to eating.

Hosting Pickling and Fermentation Workshops

Hosting pickling and fermentation workshops is a communal and educational endeavor that taps into the growing interest in traditional food preservation techniques. These workshops teach valuable skills and foster a sense of community among participants, promoting a deeper understanding of food science, sustainability, and culinary diversity. This section explores the various aspects of organizing and hosting successful pickling and fermentation workshops, from planning and preparation to execution and follow-up.

The resurgence of interest in pickling and fermentation is driven by a desire for healthier eating habits, a curiosity about traditional culinary practices, and a concern for food sustainability. Workshops that focus on these methods offer participants hands-on experience, making the processes of pickling and fermenting less intimidating and more accessible. They act as platforms for learning, sharing, and exploring the rich tapestry of flavors that fermented foods bring to the table.

The first step in hosting a workshop is planning. This involves deciding on the focus of the workshop, whether it's a general introduction to pickling and fermentation or a deep dive into specific techniques such as making sauerkraut, kimchi, kombucha, or sourdough. The workshop's scope will determine the materials needed, the duration of the session, and the level of expertise required from the instructor. It's essential to consider the target audience's interests and skill levels when planning the workshop content to make sure that it meets their requirements and expectations.

Preparation is key to the success of any workshop. This includes sourcing quality ingredients and ensuring that all necessary equipment is available and in good condition. Participants should have access to jars, cutting boards, knives, fermentation weights, and other relevant tools. It's also crucial to create a clean and safe working environment, emphasizing the importance of sanitation in the pickling and fermentation processes. Preparing detailed handouts or guides that participants can take home is an excellent way to reinforce the lessons learned during the workshop.

The execution of the workshop should be structured yet flexible, allowing for a balance between instruction and hands-on practice. A successful workshop often begins with a brief overview of the history and science of pickling and fermentation, highlighting the health benefits and sustainability aspects of these practices. The instructor's demonstration can be followed by guided practice sessions where participants get to apply what they've learned, creating their own pickled or fermented products. Encouraging questions and facilitating discussions among participants can enhance the learning experience, allowing for the exchange of tips, personal anecdotes, and cultural traditions related to pickling and fermentation.

Engagement is a critical component of any workshop. Creating an interactive and supportive environment encourages participants to experiment and share their experiences. Incorporating taste tests of various pickled and fermented foods can expand participants' palates and inspire them to explore these flavors in their cooking. Group activities or challenges, such as designing a unique pickle recipe or troubleshooting a fermentation project, can further foster camaraderie and engagement. Follow-up after the workshop is essential for reinforcing the knowledge gained and building a community of practice. Providing participants with resources, such as online forums, recipe sharing platforms, or social media groups, can keep the conversation going and offer continued support as they experiment with pickling and fermentation at home. Feedback surveys can also provide valuable insights for improving future workshops, ensuring they remain relevant and responsive to participants' interests and needs.

In conclusion, hosting pickling and fermentation workshops is a fulfilling way to spread knowledge and appreciation for these ancient culinary arts. Through careful planning, preparation, and execution, these workshops can demystify the processes of pickling and fermentation, empowering individuals to incorporate these healthful and sustainable practices into their daily lives. By fostering a sense of community and ongoing engagement, workshops can create a network of enthusiasts who share a passion for traditional food preservation methods, contributing to a broader movement towards mindful eating and food sovereignty. As interest in homemade pickles and ferments continues to grow, these workshops serve as vital platforms for education, exploration, and celebrating culinary heritage.

Sharing Recipes and Techniques with Community

The resurgence of interest in traditional food preservation methods, such as pickling and fermentation, has given rise to vibrant communities of enthusiasts keen on exploring and sharing the vast world of preserved flavors. These communities, formed both online and in-person, serve as hubs for the exchange of recipes, techniques, and experiences, promoting a culture of collaboration and learning. This section delves into the significance of sharing recipes and techniques within the community of pickling and fermentation, highlighting the benefits of such exchanges and their impact on preserving culinary heritage and promoting sustainable living.

At the core of these communities is a shared passion for the art and science of pickling and fermentation. These methods, which have been practiced for centuries across various cultures, offer a way to extend the shelf life of food, enhance its nutritional profile, and introduce complex flavors that cannot be achieved through cooking alone. The revival of these practices speaks to a broader movement towards mindful consumption, sustainability, and a desire to reconnect with traditional foodways.

Sharing recipes and techniques within these communities is critical in preserving culinary heritage. Many pickling and fermentation methods are deeply rooted in specific cultures and regions, passed down through generations as family secrets or local traditions. By documenting and sharing these recipes, enthusiasts help keep these traditions alive, ensuring they are not lost to time. Moreover, this exchange of knowledge allows for the cross-pollination of culinary traditions, encouraging innovation and the creation of new flavors that respect the past while looking toward the future.

The collaborative nature of these communities fosters an environment of continuous learning and experimentation. For beginners, access to a wealth of shared knowledge can demystify the processes of pickling and fermentation, making them more approachable and less intimidating. Experienced practitioners, on the other hand, benefit from the community's collective wisdom, discovering new techniques and troubleshooting tips that can enhance their practice. This culture of sharing encourages members to experiment with confidence, knowing they have a supportive network to turn to for advice and feedback.

Furthermore, sharing recipes and techniques within these communities promotes sustainability and reduces food waste. By teaching members how to preserve seasonal produce, these communities encourage using local and surplus fruits and vegetables, transforming them into delicious pickles and ferments that can be enjoyed year-round. This not only reduces reliance on commercially preserved foods, which often contain additives and preservatives, but also supports local agriculture and lessens the carbon footprint associated with food transportation and storage.

The impact of these communities extends beyond the practical aspects of food preservation, fostering a sense of belonging and connection among members. In an era where fast food and convenience often overshadow the joys of home cooking, pickling and fermentation communities offer a space for individuals to share their passion for food and its preparation. Workshops, potlucks, and online forums provide opportunities for social interaction, bridging geographical and cultural divides through a common interest in preserving food.

Digital platforms have been significant in the expansion and accessibility of these communities. Social media, blogs, and online forums have made sharing recipes, photos, and videos easier than ever, reaching a global audience and inspiring a new generation of enthusiasts. These platforms facilitate the exchange of information and provide a space for celebrating successes, sharing failures as learning experiences, and fostering a culture of support and encouragement.

In conclusion, sharing recipes and techniques of pickling and fermentation within the community is a testament to the enduring appeal of these ancient practices. This collaborative exchange preserves and revitalizes traditional culinary methods, promotes sustainability, fosters innovation, and builds a sense of community among practitioners. As more individuals discover the joys and benefits of pickling and fermentation, these communities will continue to grow, enriching our culinary landscape with new flavors and traditions. In embracing the collective wisdom of past and present generations, we ensure that the art of pickling and fermentation remains a vibrant and evolving part of our culinary heritage.

Personal Stories of Self-Sufficiency and Sustainability

Personal stories of self-sufficiency and sustainability with pickling and fermentation illuminate the profound impact these ancient food preservation methods can have on individuals and communities. From reducing food waste to promoting healthier eating habits and fostering a deeper connection to the natural world, these stories reveal the transformative power of embracing traditional culinary practices. This section explores the experiences of individuals who have embarked on journeys of self-sufficiency and sustainability through pickling and fermentation, highlighting the lessons learned, challenges faced, and the profound sense of fulfillment that comes from reclaiming control over one's food.

For many, the journey towards self-sufficiency and sustainability begins with a desire to live more consciously and in harmony with the environment. Pickling and fermentation offer a tangible way to reduce reliance on industrial food systems and reconnect with the rhythms of nature. By preserving seasonal produce at its peak, individuals can enjoy the flavors of each season year-round while minimizing the carbon footprint connected with food transportation and storage. For some, this journey is born out of necessity, driven by a desire to stretch limited resources and make the most of what is available.

Personal stories of self-sufficiency and sustainability often feature individuals who have embraced pickling and fermentation to reclaim control over their food. By learning how to preserve fruits and vegetables at home, these individuals gain a sense of empowerment and autonomy, no longer dependent on supermarkets or convenience foods to meet their dietary needs. This newfound self-sufficiency extends beyond the kitchen, empowering individuals to take part of their health and well-being by choosing whole, nutrient-rich foods that nourish their bodies and support their immune systems.

Moreover, pickling and fermentation catalyze creativity and innovation in the kitchen. Many individuals who embark on journeys of self-sufficiency and sustainability find themselves inspired to experiment with new flavors, ingredients, and techniques. Whether it's concocting a unique pickle recipe using garden-grown vegetables or fermenting a batch of homemade kombucha infused with seasonal fruits and herbs, these culinary adventures foster a spirit of curiosity and exploration that enriches the dining experience and brings joy to everyday life.

Personal stories of self-sufficiency and sustainability with pickling and fermentation also highlight the importance of community and shared knowledge. For many individuals, the journey towards greater self-sufficiency is not taken alone but as part of a broader community of like-minded individuals who share a passion for traditional food preservation methods. Whether through workshops, online forums, or local gatherings, these communities provide support, encouragement, and invaluable guidance as individuals navigate the challenges and joys of pickling and fermentation.

Challenges are an inevitable part of the journey towards self-sufficiency and sustainability, and personal stories often reflect the trials and tribulations faced along the way. From failed fermentation experiments to moldy pickles and botched batches of sauerkraut, these setbacks serve as valuable learning experiences, teaching individuals resilience, patience, and the importance of perseverance in the face of adversity. Moreover, they remind us that the path to self-sufficiency is not always linear but marked by trial and error, experimentation, and continuous improvement.

Despite the challenges, personal stories of self-sufficiency and sustainability with pickling and fermentation are ultimately tales of triumph and transformation. Individuals who embark on these journeys often find themselves profoundly changed in their relationship to food and outlook on life. They emerge with a deeper appreciation for the abundance of nature, a heightened sense of gratitude for the food on their plates, and a renewed commitment to living in harmony with the planet. These personal stories serve as beacons of hope and inspiration, reminding us of the power of resilience, community, and the age-old wisdom of traditional food preservation methods.

CONCLUSION

As we reach the end of our journey through "The Art of Pickling and Fermentation," we find ourselves not at a destination, but at the threshold of a new beginning. This book has been more than a mere exploration of culinary techniques; it has been a testament to the power of tradition, innovation, and sustainability to shape our lives and the world around us.

Throughout these pages, we have delved into the rich history and science behind pickling and fermentation, uncovering the age-old wisdom of our ancestors and the modern insights of food science. We have learned the art of transforming humble vegetables and fruits into tangy pickles, probiotic-rich ferments, and flavorful condiments, discovering along the way the endless possibilities for culinary creativity and exploration.

Yet, pickling and fermentation hold profound implications for our health, environment, and communities beyond the realm of taste and texture. We have explored the myriad health benefits of incorporating fermented foods into our diets, from improved digestion to enhanced immune function. We have witnessed the transformative power of these techniques in reducing food waste, preserving seasonal abundance, and promoting sustainable agriculture. And we have celebrated the role of pickling and fermentation in fostering self-sufficiency, empowering individuals to take control of their food supply and embrace a more resilient way of life.

But perhaps most importantly, "The Art of Pickling and Fermentation" has been a celebration of community — of the shared joys of gathering around a table laden with homemade pickles and ferments, of the bonds forged through the exchange of recipes and techniques, and of the collective effort to build a more sustainable future for generations to come.

As we bid farewell to these pages, let us carry forth the lessons we have learned into our everyday lives. Let us embrace the rhythm of the seasons, savoring the fleeting abundance of summer harvests and the hearty comforts of winter preserves. Let us cultivate a spirit of experimentation and creativity, daring to explore new flavor combinations and techniques that reflect our unique tastes and traditions. And let us never forget the power we hold as individuals to shape the world around us, one jar of pickles at a time.

In closing, I invite you to continue your journey of discovery and exploration, armed with the knowledge and inspiration gleaned from these pages. Whether you are a seasoned homesteader or a novice fermenter, whether you live in a bustling metropolis or a rural village, the principles of pickling and fermentation are accessible to all, offering a pathway to greater health, sustainability, and self-sufficiency.

Thank you for joining me on this adventure. May your pantry be stocked with jars of homemade goodness, your table be filled with the laughter of loved ones, as well as the simple joys of good food and good company nourish your heart.

Thank you for buying and reading/ listening to our book. If you found this book useful/ helpful please take a few minutes and leave a review on the platform where you purchased our book. Your feedback matters greatly to us.